OLD MO

HOROSCOPE AND ASTRAL DIARY

SCORPIO

OLD MOORE'S

HOROSCOPE AND ASTRAL DIARY

SCORPIO

foulsham

LONDON • NEW YORK • TORONTO • SYDNEY

foulsham

Capital Point, 33 Bath Road, Slough, Berkshire, SL1 3UF, England

Foulsham books can be found in all good bookshops and direct from www.foulsham.com

ISBN: 978-0-572-03659-1

A CIP record for this book is available from the British Library

Printed and bound by CPI Group (UK) Ltd, Croydon, CR0 4YY.

CONTENTS

INTRODUCTION

Astrology has been with us for a very long time and our fascination for the starry heavens seems to go back many thousands of years. Incised bones carrying lunar calendars have been found that are tens of thousands of years old, and our belief that the stars and planets have a bearing on our daily lives could easily be almost as ancient. Astrology was studied in all the major civilisations, and shows no signs of diminishing in popularity in the 21st century. Old Moore, a time-served veteran in astrological research, continues to monitor the zodiac and has produced the Astral Diary for 2012, tailor-made to your own astrological make-up.

Old Moore's Astral Diary is unique in its ability to get the heart of your nature and to offer you the sort of advice that might come from a trusted friend. The Diaries are structured in such a way that you can see in a day-by-day sense exactly how the planets are working for you. The diary section advises how you can get the best from upcoming situations and allows you to plan ahead successfully. There is room in the daily sections to put your own observations or even appointments, and the book is conveniently structured to stay with you throughout the year.

Whilst other popular astrology books merely deal with your astrological Sun sign, the Astral Diaries go much further. Every person on the planet is unique, and Old Moore allows you to access your individuality in a number of ways. The front section gives you the chance to work out the placement of the Moon at the time of your birth and to see how its position has set an important seal on your overall nature. Perhaps most important of all, you can use the Astral Diary to discover your Rising sign. This is the zodiac sign that was appearing over the Eastern horizon at the time of your birth, and is just as important to you as an individual as is your Sun sign.

It is the synthesis of many different astrological possibilities that makes you what you are, and with the Astral Diaries you can learn so much. How do you react to love and romance? Through the unique Venus tables and the readings that follow them, you can learn where the planet Venus was at the time of your birth. It is even possible to register when little Mercury is 'retrograde', which means that it appears to be moving backwards in space when viewed from the Earth. Mercury rules communication, so be prepared to deal with a few setbacks in this area when you see the sign ☿. The Astral Diary will be an interest and a support throughout the whole year ahead.

Old Moore extends his customary greeting to all people of the Earth and offers his age-old wishes for a happy and prosperous period ahead.

THE ESSENCE
OF SCORPIO

Exploring the Personality of Scorpio the Scorpion

(24th OCTOBER – 22nd NOVEMBER)

What's in a sign?

To say that you are a little complicated and somewhat difficult to understand is probably a great understatement. The basic reason for this lies in the peculiar nature of Scorpio rulership. In terms of the elements, your zodiac sign is a Water sign. This makes you naturally emotional, deep, somewhat reserved and ever anxious to help those around you. As a direct contrast, classical astrologers always maintained that your planetary ruler was Mars. Mars is the planet of combat and aggression, being positive and dominant under most circumstances. So it can be judged from the start that there are great contradictions within the basic Scorpio nature.

It's a fact that many people are naturally cautious of Scorpio people. Perhaps this isn't surprising. Under most circumstances you appear to be quiet and peaceful, but the situation is a little like a smoking bomb. When it comes to defending yourself, or in particular those people who you see as being important to you, there is virtually no limit to which you would refuse to go. Generally speaking our ancient ancestors were extremely wise in terms of the names they gave to the different zodiac signs. Consider the apparently diminutive and retiring scorpion. It doesn't go looking for trouble and is generally happy to remain in the shadows. However, if it is provoked, or even attacked, it will take on adversaries many times its own size. It carries a barbed sting in its tail and will strike without any additional warning if necessary.

All the same, the Scorpio reputation may be a little undeserved. Yours is one of the most compassionate and caring of all the zodiac signs. When it comes to working on behalf of humanity, especially the oppressed, the sick or the disenfranchised, you show your true mettle. You cannot stand the thought of people suffering unjustifiably, which is why many of the great social reformers and even freedom fighters had the same zodiac sign as you do.

As a Scorpio you are likely to be intuitive (some would say psychic) and under most circumstances you are more than willing to follow that little voice inside yourself that tells you how to behave in any given situation.

Scorpio resources

Your nature is so very often understated that it might be said that your greatest resource is surprise. You have the ability to shock people constantly, even those who think they understand you perfectly well. This brings us back to the creature for which your zodiac sign is named. A scorpion is diminutive – and would represent a tasty snack for any would-be predator. However, it defies logic by standing its ground and fighting back. When it does, woe betide the aggressor that refuses to take account of its presence. And so it is with you. Quiet, even reserved, you tend to get on with your work. This you do efficiently and without undue fuss, approaching each task with the same methodical attitude. People often don't even realise that you are around. And then, when they least expect it, there you are!

The ability to surprise means that you often get on in life against heavy odds. In addition you have great resilience and fortitude. It is possible for you to continue to work long and hard under circumstances that would force others to retreat. Most Scorpio people would not consider themselves to be tough – in fact quite a few are positively neurotic when it comes to matters associated with their own health. Yet you can endure hardship well and almost always win through in the end.

It's true that you may not be quite as confident as you could be. If you were, people would notice you more and that would detract from that all-important element of surprise that makes you so formidable, and which is definitely the most important weapon in your armoury. However, it is clear that your greatest resource is compassion, and on those occasions when you really allow it to show, you display yourself as being one of the most important allies to your fellow men and women.

At a practical level you are more than capable and can often be expected to perform tasks that you haven't necessarily undertaken before. You have a deep intelligence and good powers to reason things out. Most important of all is a determination that no other zodiac sign can match.

Beneath the surface

This section of an account of the typical Scorpio nature could fill an entire book in itself because you are such a complicated person. However, there are certain advantages to being a Scorpio. For example, nobody is going to run away with the idea that you are basically uncomplicated and shallow. It ought to be clear enough to the dullest observer that there is a boiling, seething volcano bubbling away beneath the surface of almost every Scorpio subject.

You are often accused of having a slightly dark view of life, and it's true that many Scorpio people enjoy a rather morbid curiosity and are fascinated by subjects that make other people shudder. At the same time you could hardly be described as being one of life's natural optimists. Part of the reason for this lies in the fact that you have been disappointed in the past and may have arrived at the conclusion that to expect the worst is often the most sensible course of action. At least that way you are likely to mitigate some of the potential depression regarding failures in the future.

Although this way of thinking is somewhat faulty, it comes so naturally to the Scorpio subject that it actually works very well, though it has to be said that it might be responsible for a tendency to hold back on occasions. Assessing the way your inner mind works is as difficult for you as it is for any outsider. Even individuals who have been friends for years will sometimes come desperately unstuck if they arrive at the conclusion that they know well what makes you tick. In the recesses of your mind you are passionate, driving, restless, dissatisfied and frequently disappointed with your own efforts. On the other hand, you have the power to make dreams into realities and are excellent at hatching plans that will benefit people far from your own circle and circumstances. Being a tireless worker on behalf of the oppressed, the fate of humanity as a whole is ever an inner concern.

When you love you do so with great width and depth. Your capacity for jealousy knows no bounds and there are times when you can be as destructive to yourself as you ever could be regarding any other individual. Yet for all this your inner mind is lofty and can soar like an eagle on occasions. If the world at large was able to fathom just one tenth of the way your inner mind actually works, people would find you even more fascinating than they do already. But perhaps it's best that they don't. The deepest recesses of Scorpio are an intense secret and will usually stay that way.

Making the best of yourself

It isn't hard to find a single word that describes the way you can make the best of yourself, especially when viewed by the world at large. That word is 'communication'. When difficulties arise in your life, especially concerning other people, it's usually because you haven't managed to get your message across, and probably because you haven't even tried to do so. There is much to your nature that is electric, powerful and magnetic. These qualities make you potentially popular and fascinating to a wealth of individuals. Hide these qualities beneath too brusque an exterior and you can seem dark and brooding.

Of course it's a fine line and one that isn't easy to walk. You are constantly worried that if you show people what really makes you tick, they will not find you interesting at all. In reality this concern is totally without foundation. There is more than enough depth about you to last several lifetimes. It doesn't matter how much you give of yourself to the world at large, there are always going to be surprises galore to follow.

Use the dynamic qualities of your nature to the full. Traditionally your ruling planet is Mars – a real go-getter of a planetary ruler and one that imbues you with tremendous power to get things done at a practical level. On the way you need to show how much you care about others. Amidst a plethora of gifts offered to you by the celestial spheres, your ability to help others is likely to be top of the list. When you are giving you are also usually approachable. For you the two go hand in hand. Avoid allowing yourself to become morose or inward looking and always strive to find simple answers to simple questions.

Stick to some sort of work that you find interesting. That can be almost anything to a Scorpio, as long as it feeds the inner you. It does need to carry a degree of diversity and should ideally have an end product that is easy to see. On your journey through life don't get carried away with daydreams – yet on the other hand avoid losing your great potential to make them come true.

The impressions you give

This is one area of your life over which you do have a great deal of control. If the adage 'what you see is what you get' turns out to be true for many signs of the zodiac, it certainly isn't the case with you. The complexity of your nature makes it difficult for even you to find 'the real Scorpio', and in any case this tends to change from day to day. However, regarding some matters there isn't any doubt at all. Firstly you are deeply magnetic and possess the ability to arouse an instinctive fascination in others. Ally this to your propensity for being very positive in your decision making and you have a potentially formidable combination.

Most people already think of you as being an extremely interesting person. Unfortunately they may also occasionally consider you to be a little cool and somewhat difficult to approach. Neither of these impressions are true, it's simply that you are quite shy at heart, and sometimes find it difficult to believe that you could be liked by certain individuals. Learn to throw this erroneous assumption out of the window, and instead, expect to be viewed positively. To do so would make all the difference and would clear the way so that your more personable side can show all the time.

Very few people who know you well could fail to realise that you care deeply, especially about the well-being of the oppressed. You have a truly noble spirit, a fact that shines through in practically everything you do – yet another reason to be noticed.

It's true that you can sometimes make your secretive quality into an art form, which those looking in from the outside might find rather difficult to deal with. This represents another outward aspect of your nature that could so easily be altered. By all means keep your secrets, though not about matters that are of no real note whatsoever. In a single phrase, try to lighten up a little. It's all you need to be almost perfect!

The way forward

It must first be held in mind that Scorpio people are complicated. That's something you simply cannot get away from, no matter how much you might try. On the one hand you can deal with practical matters almost instinctively. You are resourceful, deep thinking, intense and fascinating. On the other side of the coin you are often too fond of luxury and will frequently withdraw yourself from situations that you do not care to pursue. You can be quite stubborn and can even bear a grudge if you feel that you have been provoked.

It is suggested in astrology that no quality of nature is necessarily good or bad, it really depends on the way it is used. For example, stubbornness can be considered a terrible fault, but not if you were being awkward concerning the obvious rights of an oppressed person or group. It turns out that Scorpio has more of a potential to be 'saint or sinner' than any zodiac sign. As long as you examine your motives in any given situation, whilst at the same time trying to cultivate a degree of flexibility that is not one of your natural gifts, then you won't go far wrong.

Turn on the charm when it is necessary because it will rarely if ever let you down. Think about the way you can serve the world, but don't preach about it. Love sincerely, but don't allow jealousy to spoil things. Be constructive in your determination and don't get on your high horse when it isn't necessary. Follow these simple rules for the best chance of progress.

Of course there are many positives around to start with. You are a very loyal friend, are capable of being extremely brave and tend to be very committed to family members. At the same time you are trustworthy and can work long and hard using your own initiative. Although you sometimes worry about your health, you are more robust than most and can endure a high degree of hardship if necessary. You don't take kindly to criticism but can be flexible enough to accept it if you know it is intended for your own good.

Few people doubt your sincerity – that is, when they know what you believe. So it's important to lay your thoughts on the line right from the start. And even if you don't choose to treat the whole world as a friend, you are capable of gathering a little circle around you who would never let you down. Do make sure, however, that this 'inner group' isn't simply comprised of other Scorpios!

SCORPIO ON THE CUSP

Old Moore is often asked how astrological profiles are altered for those people born at either the beginning or the end of a zodiac sign, or, more properly, on the cusps of a sign. In the case of Scorpio this would be on the 24th of October and for two or three days after, and similarly at the end of the sign, probably from the 20th to the 22nd of November. In this year's Astral Diaries, once again, Old Moore sets out to explain the differences regarding cuspid signs.

The Libra Cusp – October 24th to 26th

You are probably generally considered to be a bright and breezy sort of character, with a great deal of enthusiasm for life. Despite this, few people would doubt that you are a shrewd operator, and that you know what you want and have a fairly good idea of how to go about getting it. Not everyone likes you as much as you would wish, but that's because the Libran side of your nature longs for popularity, while set against this is your deep Scorpio need to speak your mind, even when you know that other people might wish you did not indulge in this trait very frequently. In love, you typify the split between these two signs. On the one hand you are passionate, sincere and intense, while on the other your Libran responses can cause a certain fickle sort of affection to show sometimes, probably to the confusion of those with whom you are involved at a personal level. Nevertheless, few people would find fault with your basic nature and there isn't much doubt that your heart is in the right place.

When it comes to career matters, you have a very fortunate combination. Scorpio can sometimes be accused of lacking diplomacy, but nothing could be further from the truth with Libra. As a result, you have what it takes in terms of determination but at the same time you are capable of seeing the point of view put forward by colleagues. You tend to rise to the top of the tree and, with your mixture of raw ability and humour that most of the world approves of, you can stay there.

You won't be the sort of person to make quite as many enemies as Scorpio taken alone might do, and you need the cut and thrust of the world much more than the retiring creature after whom your zodiac sign is named. Try not to be controversial and do your best to retain a sense of humour, which is essential to your well-being. Few would doubt the fact that your heart is in the right place and your creative potential could be second to none. Most important of all, you need the self-satisfaction that comes from living in the real world.

The Sagittarius Cusp – November 20th to 22nd

You can be a really zany character, with a love of life that is second to none. Add to this a penetrating insight, a razor-sharp wit and an instinctive intuition that is quite remarkable and we find in you a formidable person. It's true that not everyone understands what makes you tick, probably least of all yourself, but you strive to be liked and really do want to advertise your willingness to learn and to grow, which isn't always the province of Scorpio when taken alone. Your capacity for work knows no bounds, though you don't really like to get your hands dirty and would feel more content when telling others what to do.

In a career sense, you need to be in a position from which you are able to delegate. This is not because you are afraid of hard work yourself, far from it, but you possess a strong ability to see through problems and you are a natural director of others. Sales careers may interest you, or a position from which you can organise and arrange things. However, you hate to be tied down to one place for long, so you would be at your best when allowed to move around freely and do things in your own way.

You are a natural social reformer, mainly because you are sure that you know what is right and just. In the main you are correct in your assumptions, but there are occasions when you should realise that there is more than one form of truth. Perhaps you are not always quite as patient with certain individuals as you might be but these generally tend to be people who show traits of cruelty or cunning. As a family person, you care very much for the people who figure most prominently in your life. Sometimes you are a definite home bird, with a preference for what you know and love, but this is offset by a restless trend within your nature that often sends you off into the wide blue yonder, chasing rainbows that the Scorpio side of your nature doubts are even there. Few would doubt your charm, your magnetism, or your desire to get ahead in life in almost any way possible. You combine patience with genuine talent and make a loyal, interesting and entertaining friend or lover.

SCORPIO AND ITS ASCENDANTS

The nature of every individual on the planet is composed of the rich variety of zodiac signs and planetary positions that were present at the time of their birth. Your Sun sign, which in your case is Scorpio, is one of the many factors when it comes to assessing the unique person you are. Probably the most important consideration, other than your Sun sign, is to establish the zodiac sign that was rising over the eastern horizon at the time that you were born. This is your Ascending or Rising sign. Most popular astrology fails to take account of the Ascendant, and yet its importance remains with you from the very moment of your birth, through every day of your life. The Ascendant is evident in the way you approach the world, and so, when meeting a person for the first time, it is this astrological influence that you are most likely to notice first. Our Ascending sign essentially represents what we appear to be, while the Sun sign is what we feel inside ourselves.

The Ascendant also has the potential for modifying our overall nature. For example, if you were born at a time of day when Scorpio was passing over the eastern horizon (this would be around the time of dawn) then you would be classed as a double Scorpio. As such, you would typify this zodiac sign, both internally and in your dealings with others. However, if your Ascendant sign turned out to be a Fire sign, such as Aries, there would be a profound alteration of nature, away from the expected qualities of Scorpio.

One of the reasons why popular astrology often ignores the Ascendant is that it has always been rather difficult to establish. Old Moore has found a way to make this possible by devising an easy-to-use table, which you will find on page 159 of this book. Using this, you can establish your Ascendant sign at a glance. You will need to know your rough time of birth, then it is simply a case of following the instructions.

For those readers who have no idea of their time of birth it might be worth allowing a good friend, or perhaps your partner, to read through the section that follows this introduction. Someone who deals with you on a regular basis may easily discover your Ascending sign, even though you could have some difficulty establishing it for yourself. A good understanding of this component of your nature is essential if you want to be aware of that 'other person' who is responsible for the way you make contact with the world at large. Your Sun sign, Ascendant sign, and the other pointers in this book will, together, allow you a far better understanding of what makes you tick as an individual. Peeling back the different layers of your astrological make-up can be an enlightening experience, and the Ascendant may represent one of the most important layers of all.

Scorpio with Scorpio Ascendant

This is one of the most potent of all astrological possibilities, but how it is used depends so very much on the individual who possesses it. On the one hand you are magnetic, alluring, sexy, deep and very attractive, whilst at the same time you are capable of being stubborn, self-seeking, vain, over-sensitive and fathomless. It has to be said that under most circumstances the first set of adjectives are the most appropriate, and that is because you keep control of the deeper side, refusing to allow it absolute control over your conscious life. You are able to get almost anything you want from life, but first you have to discover what that might be. The most important factor of all, however, is the way you can offer yourself, totally and without reservation to a needy world.

Self-sacrifice is a marvellous thing, but you can go too far on occasions. The furthest extreme for Scorpios here is a life that is totally dedicated to work and prayer. For the few this is admirable, for the still earth-based, less so. Finding a compromise is not easy as you are not always in touch with yourself. Feed the spiritual, curb the excesses, accept the need for luxury, and be happy.

Scorpio with Sagittarius Ascendant

There are many gains with this combination, and most of you reading this will already be familiar with the majority of them. Sagittarius offers a bright and hopeful approach to life, but may not always have the staying power and the patience to get what it really needs. Scorpio, on the other hand, can be too deep for its own good, is very self-seeking on occasions and extremely giving to others. Both the signs have problems when taken on their own, and, it has to be said, double the difficulties when they come together. But this is not usually the case. Invariably the presence of Scorpio slows down the over-quick responses of the Archer, whilst the inclusion of Sagittarius prevents Scorpio from taking itself too seriously.

Life is so often a game of extremes, when all the great spiritual masters of humanity have indicated that a 'middle way' is the path to choose. You have just the right combination of skills and mental faculties to find that elusive path, and can bring great joy to yourself and others as a result. Most of the time you are happy, optimistic, helpful and a joy to know. You have mental agility, backed up by a stunning intuition, which itself would rarely let you down. Keep a sense of proportion and understand that your depth of intellect is necessary to curb your flighty side.

Scorpio with Capricorn Ascendant

If patience, perseverance and a solid ability to get where you want to go are considered to be the chief components of a happy life, then you should be skipping about every day. Unfortunately this is not always the case and here we have two zodiac signs, both of which can be too deep for their own good. Both Scorpio and Capricorn are inclined to take themselves rather too seriously and your main lesson in life, and some would say the reason you have adopted this zodiac combination, is to 'lighten up'. If all that determination is pushed in the direction of your service to the world at large, you are seen as being one of the kindest people imaginable. This is really the only option for you, because if you turn this tremendous potential power inwards all the time you will become brooding, secretive and sometimes even selfish. Your eyes should be turned towards a needy humanity, which can be served with the dry but definite wit of Capricorn and the true compassion of Scorpio.

It is impossible with this combination to indicate what areas of life suit you the best. Certainly you adore luxury in all its forms, and yet you can get by with almost nothing. You desire travel, and at the same time love the comforts and stability of home. The people who know you best are aware that you are rather special. Listen to what they say.

Scorpio with Aquarius Ascendant

Here we have a combination that shows much promise and a flexibility that allows many changes in direction, allied to a power to succeed, sometimes very much against all the odds. Aquarius lightens the load of the Scorpio mind, turning the depths into potential and making intuitive foresight into a means for getting on in life. There are depths here, because even airy Aquarius isn't too easy to understand, and it is therefore a fact that some people with this combination will always be something of a mystery. However, even this fact can be turned to your advantage because it means that people will always be looking at you. Confidence is so often the key to success in life and the Scorpio–Aquarius mix offers this, or at least appears to do so. Even when this is not entirely the case, the fact that everyone around you believes it to be true is often enough.

You are usually good to know, and show a keen intellect and a deep intelligence, aided by a fascination for life that knows no bounds. When at your best you are giving, understanding, balanced and active. On those occasions when things are not going well for you, beware a stubborn streak and the need to be sensational. Keep it light and happy and you won't go far wrong. Most of you are very, very well loved.

Scorpio with Pisces Ascendant

You stand a chance of disappearing so deep into yourself that other people would need one of those long ladders that cave explorers use, just to find you. It isn't really your fault because both Scorpio and Pisces are Water signs, which are difficult to understand, and you have them both. But that doesn't mean that you should be content to remain in the dark, and the warmth of your nature is all you need to shine a light on the wonderful qualities you possess. But the primary word of warning is that you must put yourself on display and allow others to know what you are, before their appreciation of these facts becomes apparent.

As a server of the world you are second to none and it is hard to find a person with this combination who is not, in some way, looking out for the people around them. Immensely attractive to others, you are also one of the most sought-after lovers. Much of this has to do with your deep and abiding charm, but the air of mystery that surrounds you also helps. Some of you will marry too early, and end up regretting the fact, though the majority of people with Scorpio and Pisces will find the love they deserve in the end. You are able, just, firm but fair, though a sucker for a hard luck story and as kind as the day is long. It's hard to imagine how so many good points could be ignored by others.

Scorpio with Aries Ascendant

The two very different faces of Mars come together in this potent, magnetic and quite awe-inspiring combination. Your natural inclination is towards secrecy, and this fact, together with the natural attractions of the sensual Scorpio nature, makes you the object of great curiosity. This means that you will not go short of attention and should ensure that you are always being analysed by people who may never get to know you at all. At heart you prefer your own company, and yet life appears to find means to push you into the public gaze time and again. Most people with this combination ooze sex appeal and can use this fact as a stepping stone to personal success, yet without losing any integrity or loosening the cords of a deeply moralistic nature.

On those occasions when you do lose your temper, there isn't a character in the length and breadth of the zodiac who would have either the words or the courage to stand against the stream of invective that follows. On really rare occasions you might even scare yourself. A simple look is enough to show family members when you are not amused. Few people are left unmoved by your presence in their life.

Scorpio with Taurus Ascendant

The first, last and most important piece of advice for you is not to take yourself, or anyone else, too seriously. This might be rather a tall order because Scorpio intensifies the deeper qualities of Taurus and can make you rather lacking in the sense of humour that we all need to live our lives in this most imperfect of worlds. You are naturally sensual by nature. This shows itself in a host of ways. In all probability you can spend hours in the bath, love to treat yourself to good food and drink and take your greatest pleasure in neat and orderly surroundings. This can often alienate you from those who live in the same house because other people need to use the bathroom from time to time and they cannot remain tidy indefinitely.

You tend to worry a great deal about things which are really not too important, but don't take this statement too seriously or you will begin to worry about this fact too! You often need to lighten up and should always do your best to tell yourself that most things are not half so important as they seem to be. Be careful over the selection of a life partner and if possible choose someone who is naturally funny and who does not take life anywhere near as seriously as you are inclined to do. At work you are more than capable and in all probability everyone relies heavily on your wise judgements.

Scorpio with Gemini Ascendant

What you are and what you appear to be can be two entirely different things with this combination. Although you appear to be every bit as chatty and even as flighty as Gemini tends to be, nothing could be further from the truth. In reality you have many deep and penetrating insights, all of which are geared towards sorting out potential problems before they come along. Few people would have the ability to pull the wool over your eyes, and you show a much more astute face to the world than is often the case for Gemini taken on its own. The level of your confidence, although not earth-shattering, is much greater with this combination, and you would not be thwarted once you had made up your mind.

There is a slight danger here, however, because Gemini is always inclined to nerve problems of one sort or another. In the main these are slight and fleeting, though the presence of Scorpio can intensify reactions and heighten the possibility of depression, which would not be at all fortunate. The best way round this potential problem is to have a wealth of friends, plenty to do and the sort of variety in your life that suits your Mercury ruler. Financial success is not too difficult to achieve because you can easily earn money and then manage to hold on to it.

Scorpio with Cancer Ascendant

There are few more endearing zodiac combinations than this one. Both signs are Watery in nature and show a desire to work on behalf of humanity as a whole. The world sees you as being genuinely caring, full of sympathy for anyone in trouble and always ready to lend a hand when it is needed. You are a loyal friend, a great supporter of the oppressed and a lover of home and family. In a work sense you are capable, and command respect from your colleagues, even though this comes about courtesy of your quiet competence and not as a result of anything that you might happen to say.

But we should not get too carried away with external factors, or the way that others see you. Inside you are a boiling pool of emotion. You feel more strongly, love more deeply and hurt more fully than any other combination of the Water signs. Even those who think they know you really well would get a shock if they could take a stroll around the deeper recesses of your mind. Although these facts are true, they may be rather beside the point because it is a fact that the truth of your passion, commitment and deep convictions may only surface fully half a dozen times in your life. The fact is that you are a very private person at heart and you don't know how to be any other way.

Scorpio with Leo Ascendant

A Leo with intensity, that's what you are. You are mad about good causes and would argue the hind leg off a donkey in defence of your many ideals. If you are not out there saving the planet you could just be at home in the bath, thinking up the next way to save humanity from its own worst excesses. In your own life, although you love little luxuries, you are sparing and frugal, yet generous as can be to those you take to. It's a fact that you don't like everyone, and of course the same is true in reverse. It might be easier for you to understand why you can dislike than to appreciate the reverse side of the coin, for your pride can be badly dented on occasions. Scorpio brings a tendency to have down spells, though the fact that Leo is also strongly represented in your nature should prevent them from becoming a regular part of your life.

It is important for you to learn how to forgive and forget, and there isn't much point in bearing a grudge because you are basically too noble to do so. If something goes wrong, kiss the situation goodbye and get on with the next interesting adventure, of which there are many in your life. Stop–start situations sometimes get in the way, but there are plenty of people around who would be only too willing to lend a helping hand.

Scorpio with Virgo Ascendant

This is intensity carried through to the absolute. If you have a problem, it is that you fail to externalise all that is going on inside that deep, bubbling cauldron that is your inner self. Realising what you are capable of is not a problem; these only start when you have to make it plain to those around you what you want. Part of the reason for this is that you don't always understand yourself. You love intensely and would do absolutely anything for a person you are fond of, even though you might have to inconvenience yourself a great deal on the way. Relationships can cause you slight problems however, since you need to associate with people who at least come somewhere near to understanding what makes you tick. If you manage to bridge the gap between yourself and the world that constantly knocks on your door, you show yourself to be powerful, magnetic and compulsive.

There are times when you definitely prefer to stay quiet, though you do have a powerful ability to get your message across when you think it is necessary to do so. There are people around who might think that you are a push-over but they could easily get a shock when you sense that the time is right to answer back. You probably have a very orderly house and don't care for clutter of any sort.

Scorpio with Libra Ascendant

There is some tendency for you to be far more deep than the average Libran would appear to be and for this reason it is crucial that you lighten up from time to time. Every person with a Scorpio quality needs to remember that there is a happy and carefree side to all events and your Libran quality should allow you to bear this in mind. Sometimes you try to do too many things at the same time. This is fine if you take the casual overview of Libra, but less sensible when you insist on picking the last bone out of every potential, as is much more the case for Scorpio.

When worries come along, as they sometimes will, be able to listen to what your friends have to say and also realise that they are more than willing to work on your behalf, if only because you are so loyal to them. You do have a quality of self-deception, but this should not get in the way too much if you combine the instinctive actions of Libra with the deep intuition of your Scorpio component.

Probably the most important factor of this combination is your ability to succeed in a financial sense. You make a good manager, but not of the authoritarian sort. Jobs in the media or where you are expected to make up your mind quickly would suit you, because there is always an underpinning of practical sense that rarely lets you down.

THE MOON AND THE PART IT PLAYS IN YOUR LIFE

In astrology the Moon is probably the single most important heavenly body after the Sun. Its unique position, as partner to the Earth on its journey around the solar system, means that the Moon appears to pass through the signs of the zodiac extremely quickly. The zodiac position of the Moon at the time of your birth plays a great part in personal character and is especially significant in the build-up of your emotional nature.

Sun Moon Cycles

The first lunar cycle deals with the part the position of the Moon plays relative to your Sun sign. I have made the fluctuations of this pattern easy for you to understand by means of a simple cyclic graph. It appears on the first page of each 'Your Month At A Glance', under the title 'Highs and Lows'. The graph displays the lunar cycle and you will soon learn to understand how its movements have a bearing on your level of energy and your abilities.

Your Own Moon Sign

Discovering the position of the Moon at the time of your birth has always been notoriously difficult because tracking the complex zodiac positions of the Moon is not easy. This process has been reduced to three simple stages with Old Moore's unique Lunar Tables. A breakdown of the Moon's zodiac positions can be found from page 25 onwards, so that once you know what your Moon Sign is, you can see what part this plays in the overall build-up of your personal character.

If you follow the instructions on the next page you will soon be able to work out exactly what zodiac sign the Moon occupied on the day that you were born and you can then go on to compare the reading for this position with those of your Sun sign and your Ascendant. It is partly the comparison between these three important positions that goes towards making you the unique individual you are.

HOW TO DISCOVER YOUR MOON SIGN

This is a three-stage process. You may need a pen and a piece of paper but if you follow the instructions below the process should only take a minute or so.

STAGE 1 First of all you need to know the Moon Age at the time of your birth. If you look at Moon Table 1, on page 23, you will find all the years between 1914 and 2012 down the left side. Find the year of your birth and then trace across to the right to the month of your birth. Where the two intersect you will find a number. This is the date of the New Moon in the month that you were born. You now need to count forward the number of days between the New Moon and your own birthday. For example, if the New Moon in the month of your birth was shown as being the 6th and you were born on the 20th, your Moon Age Day would be 14. If the New Moon in the month of your birth came after your birthday, you need to count forward from the New Moon in the previous month. Whatever the result, jot this number down so that you do not forget it.

STAGE 2 Take a look at Moon Table 2 on page 24. Down the left hand column look for the date of your birth. Now trace across to the month of your birth. Where the two meet you will find a letter. Copy this letter down alongside your Moon Age Day.

STAGE 3 Moon Table 3 on page 24 will supply you with the zodiac sign the Moon occupied on the day of your birth. Look for your Moon Age Day down the left hand column and then for the letter you found in Stage 2. Where the two converge you will find a zodiac sign and this is the sign occupied by the Moon on the day that you were born.

Your Zodiac Moon Sign Explained

You will find a profile of all zodiac Moon Signs on pages 25 to 28, showing in yet another way how astrology helps to make you into the individual that you are. In each daily entry of the Astral Diary you can find the zodiac position of the Moon for every day of the year. This also allows you to discover your lunar birthdays. Since the Moon passes through all the signs of the zodiac in about a month, you can expect something like twelve lunar birthdays each year. At these times you are likely to be emotionally steady and able to make the sort of decisions that have real, lasting value.

MOON TABLE 1

YEAR	SEP	OCT	NOV	YEAR	SEP	OCT	NOV	YEAR	SEP	OCT	NOV
1914	19	19	17	1947	14	14	12	1980	10	9	8
1915	9	8	7	1948	3	2	1	1981	28	27	26
1916	27	27	26	1949	23	21	20	1982	17	17	15
1917	15	15	14	1950	12	11	9	1983	7	6	4
1918	4	4	3	1951	1	1/30	29	1984	25	24	22
1919	23	23	22	1952	19	18	17	1985	14	14	12
1920	12	12	10	1953	8	8	6	1986	4	3	2
1921	2	1/30	29	1954	27	26	25	1987	23	22	21
1922	21	20	19	1955	16	15	14	1988	11	10	9
1923	10	10	8	1956	4	4	2	1989	29	29	28
1924	28	28	26	1957	23	23	21	1990	19	18	17
1925	18	17	16	1958	13	12	11	1991	8	8	6
1926	7	6	5	1959	3	2/31	30	1992	26	25	24
1927	25	25	24	1960	21	20	19	1993	16	15	14
1928	14	14	12	1961	10	9	8	1994	5	5	3
1929	3	2	1	1962	28	28	27	1995	24	24	22
1930	22	20	19	1963	17	17	15	1996	13	11	10
1931	12	11	9	1964	6	5	4	1997	2	2/31	30
1932	30	29	27	1965	25	24	22	1998	20	20	19
1933	19	19	17	1966	14	14	12	1999	9	9	8
1934	9	8	7	1967	4	3	2	2000	27	27	26
1935	27	27	26	1968	23	22	21	2001	17	17	16
1936	15	15	14	1969	11	10	9	2002	6	6	4
1937	4	4	3	1970	1	1/30	29	2003	26	25	24
1938	23	23	22	1971	19	19	18	2004	13	12	11
1939	13	12	11	1972	8	8	6	2005	3	2	1
1940	2	1/30	29	1973	27	26	25	2006	22	21	20
1941	21	20	19	1974	16	15	14	2007	12	11	9
1942	10	10	8	1975	5	5	3	2008	30	29	28
1943	29	29	27	1976	23	23	21	2009	19	18	17
1944	17	17	15	1977	13	12	11	2010	8	8	6
1945	6	6	4	1978	2	2/31	30	2011	27	27	25
1946	25	24	23	1979	21	20	19	2012	6	15	13

TABLE 2

DAY	OCT	NOV
1	a	e
2	a	e
3	a	e
4	b	f
5	b	f
6	b	f
7	b	f
8	b	f
9	b	f
10	b	f
11	b	f
12	b	f
13	b	g
14	d	g
15	d	g
16	d	g
17	d	g
18	d	g
19	d	g
20	d	g
21	d	g
22	d	g
23	d	i
24	e	i
25	e	i
26	e	i
27	e	i
28	e	i
29	e	i
30	e	i
31	e	–

TABLE 3

M/D	a	b	d	e	f	g	i
0	LI	LI	LI	SC	SC	SC	SA
1	LI	LI	SC	SC	SC	SA	SA
2	LI	SC	SC	SC	SA	SA	CP
3	SC	SC	SC	SA	SA	CP	CP
4	SC	SA	SA	SA	CP	CP	CP
5	SA	SA	SA	CP	CP	AQ	AQ
6	SA	CP	CP	CP	AQ	AQ	AQ
7	SA	CP	CP	AQ	AQ	PI	PI
8	CP	CP	CP	AQ	PI	PI	PI
9	CP	AQ	AQ	AQ	PI	PI	AR
10	AQ	AQ	AQ	PI	AR	AR	AR
11	AQ	PI	PI	PI	AR	AR	TA
12	PI	PI	PI	AR	TA	TA	TA
13	PI	AR	PI	AR	TA	TA	GE
14	AR	AR	AR	TA	GE	GE	GE
15	AR	AR	AR	TA	TA	TA	GE
16	AR	AR	TA	TA	GE	GE	GE
17	AR	TA	TA	GE	GE	GE	CA
18	TA	TA	GE	GE	GE	CA	CA
19	TA	TA	GE	GE	CA	CA	CA
20	GE	GE	GE	CA	CA	CA	LE
21	GE	GE	CA	CA	CA	LE	LE
22	GE	CA	CA	CA	LE	LE	VI
23	CA	CA	CA	LE	LE	LE	VI
24	CA	CA	LE	LE	LE	VI	VI
25	CA	LE	LE	LE	VI	VI	LI
26	LE	LE	VI	VI	VI	LI	LI
27	LE	VI	VI	VI	LI	LI	SC
28	VI	VI	VI	LI	LI	LI	SC
29	VI	VI	LI	LI	LI	SC	SC

AR = Aries, TA = Taurus, GE = Gemini, CA = Cancer, LE = Leo, VI = Virgo, LI = Libra, SC = Scorpio, SA = Sagittarius, CP = Capricorn, AQ = Aquarius, PI = Pisces

MOON SIGNS

Moon in Aries

You have a strong imagination, courage, determination and a desire to do things in your own way and forge your own path through life.

Originality is a key attribute; you are seldom stuck for ideas although your mind is changeable and you could take the time to focus on individual tasks. Often quick-tempered, you take orders from few people and live life at a fast pace. Avoid health problems by taking regular time out for rest and relaxation.

Emotionally, it is important that you talk to those you are closest to and work out your true feelings. Once you discover that people are there to help, there is less necessity for you to do everything yourself.

Moon in Taurus

The Moon in Taurus gives you a courteous and friendly manner, which means you are likely to have many friends.

The good things in life mean a lot to you, as Taurus is an Earth sign that delights in experiences which please the senses. Hence you are probably a lover of good food and drink, which may in turn mean you need to keep an eye on the bathroom scales, especially as looking good is also important to you.

Emotionally you are fairly stable and you stick by your own standards. Taureans do not respond well to change. Intuition also plays an important part in your life.

Moon in Gemini

You have a warm-hearted character, sympathetic and eager to help others. At times reserved, you can also be articulate and chatty: this is part of the paradox of Gemini, which always brings duplicity to the nature. You are interested in current affairs, have a good intellect, and are good company and likely to have many friends. Most of your friends have a high opinion of you and would be ready to defend you should the need arise. However, this is usually unnecessary, as you are quite capable of defending yourself in any verbal confrontation.

Travel is important to your inquisitive mind and you find intellectual stimulus in mixing with people from different cultures. You also gain much from reading, writing and the arts but you do need plenty of rest and relaxation in order to avoid fatigue.

Moon in Cancer

The Moon in Cancer at the time of birth is a fortunate position as Cancer is the Moon's natural home. This means that the qualities of compassion and understanding given by the Moon are especially enhanced in your nature, and you are friendly and sociable and cope well with emotional pressures. You cherish home and family life, and happily do the domestic tasks. Your surroundings are important to you and you hate squalor and filth. You are likely to have a love of music and poetry.

Your basic character, although at times changeable like the Moon itself, depends on symmetry. You aim to make your surroundings comfortable and harmonious, for yourself and those close to you.

Moon in Leo

The best qualities of the Moon and Leo come together to make you warmhearted, fair, ambitious and self-confident. With good organisational abilities, you invariably rise to a position of responsibility in your chosen career. This is fortunate as you don't enjoy being an 'also-ran' and would rather be an important part of a small organisation than a menial in a large one.

You should be lucky in love, and happy, provided you put in the effort to make a comfortable home for yourself and those close to you. It is likely that you will have a love of pleasure, sport, music and literature. Life brings you many rewards, most of them as a direct result of your own efforts, although you may be luckier than average and ready to make the best of any situation.

Moon in Virgo

You are endowed with good mental abilities and a keen receptive memory, but you are never ostentatious or pretentious. Naturally quite reserved, you still have many friends, especially of the opposite sex. Marital relationships must be discussed carefully and worked at so that they remain harmonious, as personal attachments can be a problem if you do not give them your full attention.

Talented and persevering, you possess artistic qualities and are a good homemaker. Earning your honours through genuine merit, you work long and hard towards your objectives but show little pride in your achievements. Many short journeys will be undertaken in your life.

Moon in Libra

With the Moon in Libra you are naturally popular and make friends easily. People like you, probably more than you realise, you bring fun to a party and are a natural diplomat. For all its good points, Libra is not the most stable of astrological signs and, as a result, your emotions can be a little unstable too. Therefore, although the Moon in Libra is said to be good for love and marriage, your Sun sign and Rising sign will have an important effect on your emotional and loving qualities.

You must remember to relate to others in your decision-making. Co-operation is crucial because Libra represents the 'balance' of life that can only be achieved through harmonious relationships. Conformity is not easy for you because Libra, an Air sign, likes its independence.

Moon in Scorpio

Some people might call you pushy. In fact, all you really want to do is to live life to the full and protect yourself and your family from the pressures of life. Take care to avoid giving the impression of being sarcastic or impulsive and use your energies wisely and constructively.

You have great courage and you invariably achieve your goals by force of personality and sheer effort. You are fond of mystery and are good at predicting the outcome of situations and events. Travel experiences can be beneficial to you.

You may experience problems if you do not take time to examine your motives in a relationship, and also if you allow jealousy, always a feature of Scorpio, to cloud your judgement.

Moon in Sagittarius

The Moon in Sagittarius helps to make you a generous individual with humanitarian qualities and a kind heart. Restlessness may be intrinsic as your mind is seldom still. Perhaps because of this, you have a need for change that could lead you to several major moves during your adult life. You are not afraid to stand your ground when you know your judgement is right, you speak directly and have good intuition.

At work you are quick, efficient and versatile and so you make an ideal employee. You need work to be intellectually demanding and do not enjoy tedious routines.

In relationships, you anger quickly if faced with stupidity or deception, though you are just as quick to forgive and forget. Emotionally, there are times when your heart rules your head.

Moon in Capricorn

The Moon in Capricorn makes you popular and likely to come into the public eye in some way. The watery Moon is not entirely comfortable in the Earth sign of Capricorn and this may lead to some difficulties in the early years of life. An initial lack of creative ability and indecision must be overcome before the true qualities of patience and perseverance inherent in Capricorn can show through.

You have good administrative ability and are a capable worker, and if you are careful you can accumulate wealth. But you must be cautious and take professional advice in partnerships, as you are open to deception. You may be interested in social or welfare work, which suit your organisational skills and sympathy for others.

Moon in Aquarius

The Moon in Aquarius makes you an active and agreeable person with a friendly, easy-going nature. Sympathetic to the needs of others, you flourish in a laid-back atmosphere. You are broad-minded, fair and open to suggestion, although sometimes you have an unconventional quality which others can find hard to understand.

You are interested in the strange and curious, and in old articles and places. You enjoy trips to these places and gain much from them. Political, scientific and educational work interests you and you might choose a career in science or technology.

Money-wise, you make gains through innovation and concentration and Lunar Aquarians often tackle more than one job at a time. In love you are kind and honest.

Moon in Pisces

You have a kind, sympathetic nature, somewhat retiring at times, but you always take account of others' feelings and help when you can.

Personal relationships may be problematic, but as life goes on you can learn from your experiences and develop a better understanding of yourself and the world around you.

You have a fondness for travel, appreciate beauty and harmony and hate disorder and strife. You may be fond of literature and would make a good writer or speaker yourself. You have a creative imagination and may come across as an incurable romantic. You have strong intuition, maybe bordering on a mediumistic quality, which sets you apart from the mass. You may not be rich in cash terms, but your personal gifts are worth more than gold.

SCORPIO IN LOVE

Discover how compatible you are with people from the same and other parts of the zodiac. Five stars equals a match made in heaven!

Scorpio meets Scorpio

Scorpio is deep, complex and enigmatic, traits which often lead to misunderstanding with other zodiac signs, so a double Scorpio match can work well because both parties understand one another. They will allow each other periods of silence and reflection but still be willing to help, advise and support when necessary. Their relationship may seem odd to others but that doesn't matter if those involved are happy. All in all, an unusual but contented combination. Star rating: *****

Scorpio meets Sagittarius

Sagittarius needs constant stimulation and loves to be busy from dawn till dusk which may mean that it feels rather frustrated by Scorpio. Scorpions are hard workers, too, but they are also contemplative and need periods of quiet which may mean that they appear dull to Sagittarius. This could lead to a gulf between the two which must be overcome. With time and patience on both sides, this can be a lucrative encounter and good in terms of home and family. A variable alliance. Star rating: ***

Scorpio meets Capricorn

Lack of communication is the governing factor here. Neither of this pair are renowned communicators and both need a partner to draw out their full verbal potential. Consequently, Scorpio may find Capricorn cold and unapproachable while Capricorn could find Scorpio dark and brooding. Both are naturally tidy and would keep a pristine house but great effort and a mutual goal is needed on both sides to overcome the missing spark. A good match on the financial side, but probably not an earthshattering personal encounter. Star rating: **

Scorpio meets Aquarius

This is a promising and practical combination. Scorpio responds well to Aquarius' exploration of its deep nature and so this shy sign becomes lighter, brighter and more inspirational. Meanwhile, Aquarians are rarely as sure of themselves as they like to appear and are reassured by Scorpio's steady and determined support. Both signs want to be kind to the other which is a basis for a relationship that should be warm most of the time and extremely hot occasionally. Star rating: ****

Scorpio meets Pisces

If ever there were two zodiac signs that have a total rapport, it has to be Scorpio and Pisces. They share very similar needs: they are not gregarious and are happy with a little silence, good music and time to contemplate the finer things in life, and both are attracted to family life. Apart, they can have a tendency to wander in a romantic sense, but this is reduced when they come together. They are deep, firm friends who enjoy each other's company and this must lead to an excellent chance of success. These people are surely made for each other! Star rating: *****

Scorpio meets Aries

There can be great affection here, even if the two signs are so very different. The common link is the planet Mars, which plays a part in both these natures. Although Aries is, outwardly, the most dominant, Scorpio people are among the most powerful to be found anywhere. This quiet determination is respected by Aries. Aries will satisfy the passionate side of Scorpio, particularly with instruction from Scorpio. There are mysteries here which will add spice to life. The few arguments that do occur are likely to be awe-inspiring. Star rating: ****

Scorpio meets Taurus

Scorpio is deep – very deep – which may be a problem, because Taurus doesn't wear its heart on its sleeve either. It might be difficult for this pair to get together, because neither is naturally inclined to make the first move. Taurus stands in awe of the power and intensity of the Scorpio mind, while the Scorpion is interested in the Bull's affable and friendly qualities, so an enduring relationship could be forged if the couple ever get round to talking. Both are lovers of home and family, which will help to cement a relationship. Star rating: **

Scorpio meets Gemini

There could be problems here. Scorpio is one of the deepest and least understood of all the zodiac signs, which at first seems like a challenge to intellectual Gemini, who thinks it can solve anything. But the deeper the Gemini digs, the further down Scorpio goes. Meanwhile, Scorpio may be finding Gemini thoughtless, shallow and even downright annoying. Gemini is often afraid of Scorpio's perception and strength, together with the sting in the Scorpion's tail. Anything is possible, but the outlook for this match is less than promising. Star rating: **

Scorpio meets Cancer

This match is potentially a great success, a fact which is often a mystery to astrologers. Some feel it is due to the compatibility of the Water element, but it could also come from a mixture of similarity and difference in the personalities. Scorpio is partly ruled by Mars, which gives it a deep, passionate, dominant and powerful side. Cancerians generally like and respect this amalgam, and recognise something there that they would like to adopt themselves. On the other side of the coin, Scorpio needs love and emotional security which Cancer offers generously. Star rating: *****

Scorpio meets Leo

Stand back and watch the sparks fly! Scorpio has the deep sensitivity of a Water sign but it is also partially ruled by Fire planet Mars, from which it draws great power, and Leo will find that difficult. Leo loves to take charge and really hates to feel psychologically undermined, which is Scorpio's stock-in-trade. Scorpio may find Leo's ideals a little shallow, which will be upsetting to the Lion. Anything is possible, but this possibility is rather slimmer than most. Star rating: **

Scorpio meets Virgo

There are one or two potential difficulties here, but there is also a meeting point from which to overcome them. Virgo is very caring and protective, a trait which Scorpio understands and even emulates. Scorpio will impress Virgo with its serious side. Both signs are consistent, although also sarcastic. Scorpio may uncover a hidden passion in Virgo which all too often lies deep within its Earth-sign nature. Material success is very likely, with Virgo taking the lion's share of the domestic chores and family responsibilities. Star rating: ***

Scorpio meets Libra

Many astrologers have reservations about this match because, on the surface, the signs are so different. However, this couple may find fulfilment because these differences mean that their respective needs are met. Scorpio needs a partner to lighten the load, which won't daunt Libra, while Libra looks for a steadfast quality which it doesn't possess, but which Scorpio can supply naturally. Financial success is possible because they both have good ideas and back them up with hard work and determination. All in all, a promising outlook. Star rating: ****

VENUS:
THE PLANET OF LOVE

If you look up at the sky around sunset or sunrise you will often see Venus in close attendance to the Sun. It is arguably one of the most beautiful sights of all and there is little wonder that historically it became associated with the goddess of love. But although Venus does play an important part in the way you view love and in the way others see you romantically, this is only one of the spheres of influence that it enjoys in your overall character.

Venus has a part to play in the more cultured side of your life and has much to do with your appreciation of art, literature, music and general creativity. Even the way you look is responsive to the part of the zodiac that Venus occupied at the start of your life, though this fact is also down to your Sun sign and Ascending sign. If, at the time you were born, Venus occupied one of the more gregarious zodiac signs, you will be more likely to wear your heart on your sleeve, as well as to be more attracted to entertainment, social gatherings and good company. If on the other hand Venus occupied a quiet zodiac sign at the time of your birth, you would tend to be more retiring and less willing to shine in public situations.

It's good to know what part the planet Venus plays in your life for it can have a great bearing on the way you appear to the rest of the world and since we all have to mix with others, you can learn to make the very best of what Venus has to offer you.

One of the great complications in the past has always been trying to establish exactly what zodiac position Venus enjoyed when you were born because the planet is notoriously difficult to track. However, I have solved that problem by creating a table that is exclusive to your Sun sign, which you will find on the following page.

Establishing your Venus sign could not be easier. Just look up the year of your birth on the page opposite and you will see a sign of the zodiac. This was the sign that Venus occupied in the period covered by your sign in that year. If Venus occupied more than one sign during the period, this is indicated by the date on which the sign changed, and the name of the new sign. For instance, if you were born in 1950, Venus was in Libra until the 28th October, after which time it was in Scorpio. If you were born before 28th October your Venus sign is Libra, if you were born on or after 28th October, your Venus sign is Scorpio. Once you have established the position of Venus at the time of your birth, you can then look in the pages which follow to see how this has a bearing on your life as a whole.

1914 SAGITTARIUS / 16.11 SCORPIO	1964 VIRGO / 31.10 LIBRA
1915 SCORPIO / 9.11 SAGITTARIUS	1965 SAGITTARIUS / 6.11 CAPRICORN
1916 VIRGO / 3.11 LIBRA	1966 LIBRA / 27.10 SCORPIO
1917 SAGITTARIUS / 7.11 CAPRICORN	1967 VIRGO / 10.11 LIBRA
1918 LIBRA / 30.10 SCORPIO	1968 SAGITTARIUS / 15.11 CAPRICORN
1919 VIRGO / 9.11 LIBRA	
1920 SCORPIO / 24.10 SAGITTARIUS / 17.11 CAPRICORN	1969 LIBRA / 11.11 SCORPIO
	1970 SAGITTARIUS / 28.10 SCORPIO
1921 LIBRA / 14.11 SCORPIO	1971 SCORPIO / 4.11 SAGITTARIUS
1922 SAGITTARIUS / 16.11 SCORPIO	1972 VIRGO / 31.10 LIBRA
1923 SCORPIO / 9.11 SAGITTARIUS	1973 SAGITTARIUS / 6.11 CAPRICORN
1924 VIRGO / 3.11 LIBRA	1974 LIBRA / 26.10 SCORPIO
1925 SAGITTARIUS / 7.11 CAPRICORN	1975 VIRGO / 9.11 LIBRA
1926 LIBRA / 29.10 SCORPIO	1976 SAGITTARIUS / 15.11 CAPRICORN
1927 VIRGO / 10.11 LIBRA	
1928 SAGITTARIUS / 17.11 CAPRICORN	1977 LIBRA / 11.11 SCORPIO
	1978 SAGITTARIUS / 28.10 SCORPIO
1929 LIBRA / 13.11 SCORPIO	1979 SCORPIO / 4.11 SAGITTARIUS
1930 SAGITTARIUS / 16.11 SCORPIO	1980 VIRGO / 30.10 LIBRA
1931 SCORPIO / 8.11 SAGITTARIUS	1981 SAGITTARIUS / 5.11 CAPRICORN
1932 VIRGO / 2.11 LIBRA	1982 LIBRA / 26.10 SCORPIO
1933 SAGITTARIUS / 7.11 CAPRICORN	1983 VIRGO / 9.11 LIBRA
1934 LIBRA / 29.10 SCORPIO	1984 SAGITTARIUS / 14.11 CAPRICORN
1935 VIRGO / 10.11 LIBRA	
1936 SAGITTARIUS / 16.11 CAPRICORN	1985 LIBRA / 10.11 SCORPIO
	1986 SAGITTARIUS / 28.10 SCORPIO
1937 LIBRA / 13.11 SCORPIO	1987 SCORPIO / 3.11 SAGITTARIUS
1938 SAGITTARIUS / 16.11 SCORPIO	1988 VIRGO / 30.10 LIBRA
1939 SCORPIO / 7.11 SAGITTARIUS	1989 SAGITTARIUS / 5.11 CAPRICORN
1940 VIRGO / 2.11 LIBRA	1990 LIBRA / 25.10 SCORPIO
1941 SAGITTARIUS / 7.11 CAPRICORN	1991 VIRGO / 9.11 LIBRA
1942 LIBRA / 28.10 SCORPIO	1992 SAGITTARIUS / 14.11 CAPRICORN
1943 VIRGO / 10.11 LIBRA	
1944 SAGITTARIUS / 16.11 CAPRICORN	1993 LIBRA / 10.11 SCORPIO
	1994 SAGITTARIUS / 28.10 SCORPIO
1945 LIBRA / 13.11 SCORPIO	1995 SCORPIO / 3.11 SAGITTARIUS
1946 SAGITTARIUS / 16.11 SCORPIO	1996 VIRGO / 29.10 LIBRA
1947 SCORPIO / 6.11 SAGITTARIUS	1997 SAGITTARIUS / 5.11 CAPRICORN
1948 VIRGO / 1.11 LIBRA	1998 LIBRA / 25.10 SCORPIO
1949 SAGITTARIUS / 6.11 CAPRICORN	1999 VIRGO / 9.11 LIBRA
1950 LIBRA / 28.10 SCORPIO	2000 SAGITTARIUS / 14.11 CAPRICORN
1951 VIRGO / 10.11 LIBRA	
1952 SAGITTARIUS / 16.11 CAPRICORN	2001 LIBRA / 10.11 SCORPIO
	2002 SAGITTARIUS / 28.10 SCORPIO
1953 LIBRA / 12.11 SCORPIO	2003 SCORPIO / 3.11 SAGITTARIUS
1954 SAGITTARIUS / 28.10 SCORPIO	2004 VIRGO / 29.10 LIBRA
1955 SCORPIO / 6.11 SAGITTARIUS	2005 SAGITTARIUS / 5.11 CAPRICORN
1956 VIRGO / 1.11 LIBRA	2006 LIBRA / 25.10 SCORPIO
1957 SAGITTARIUS / 6.11 CAPRICORN	2007 VIRGO / 9.11 LIBRA
1958 LIBRA / 27.10 SCORPIO	2008 SAGITTARIUS / 14.11 CAPRICORN
1959 VIRGO / 10.11 LIBRA	
1960 SAGITTARIUS / 15.11 CAPRICORN	2009 LIBRA / 10.11 SCORPIO
	2010 SAGITTARIUS / 28.10 SCORPIO
1961 LIBRA / 12.11 SCORPIO	2011 SCORPIO / 3.11 SAGITTARIUS
1962 SAGITTARIUS / 28.10 SCORPIO	2012 VIRGO / 29.10 LIBRA
1963 SCORPIO / 5.11 SAGITTARIUS	

VENUS THROUGH THE ZODIAC SIGNS

Venus in Aries

Amongst other things, the position of Venus in Aries indicates a fondness for travel, music and all creative pursuits. Your nature tends to be affectionate and you would try not to create confusion or difficulty for others if it could be avoided. Many people with this planetary position have a great love of the theatre, and mental stimulation is of the greatest importance. Early romantic attachments are common with Venus in Aries, so it is very important to establish a genuine sense of romantic continuity. Early marriage is not recommended, especially if it is based on sympathy. You may give your heart a little too readily on occasions.

Venus in Taurus

You are capable of very deep feelings and your emotions tend to last for a very long time. This makes you a trusting partner and lover, whose constancy is second to none. In life you are precise and careful and always try to do things the right way. Although this means an ordered life, which you are comfortable with, it can also lead you to be rather too fussy for your own good. Despite your pleasant nature, you are very fixed in your opinions and quite able to speak your mind. Others are attracted to you and historical astrologers always quoted this position of Venus as being very fortunate in terms of marriage. However, if you find yourself involved in a failed relationship, it could take you a long time to trust again.

Venus in Gemini

As with all associations related to Gemini, you tend to be quite versatile, anxious for change and intelligent in your dealings with the world at large. You may gain money from more than one source but you are equally good at spending it. There is an inference here that you are a good communicator, via either the written or the spoken word, and you love to be in the company of interesting people. Always on the look-out for culture, you may also be very fond of music, and love to indulge the curious and cultured side of your nature. In romance you tend to have more than one relationship and could find yourself associated with someone who has previously been a friend or even a distant relative.

Venus in Cancer

You often stay close to home because you are very fond of family and enjoy many of your most treasured moments when you are with those you love. Being naturally sympathetic, you will always do anything you can to support those around you, even people you hardly know at all. This charitable side of your nature is your most noticeable trait and is one of the reasons why others are naturally so fond of you. Being receptive and in some cases even psychic, you can see through to the soul of most of those with whom you come into contact. You may not commence too many romantic attachments but when you do give your heart, it tends to be unconditionally.

Venus in Leo

It must become quickly obvious to almost anyone you meet that you are kind, sympathetic and yet determined enough to stand up for anyone or anything that is truly important to you. Bright and sunny, you warm the world with your natural enthusiasm and would rarely do anything to hurt those around you, or at least not intentionally. In romance you are ardent and sincere, though some may find your style just a little overpowering. Gains come through your contacts with other people and this could be especially true with regard to romance, for love and money often come hand in hand for those who were born with Venus in Leo. People claim to understand you, though you are more complex than you seem.

Venus in Virgo

Your nature could well be fairly quiet no matter what your Sun sign might be, though this fact often manifests itself as an inner peace and would not prevent you from being basically sociable. Some delays and even the odd disappointment in love cannot be ruled out with this planetary position, though it's a fact that you will usually find the happiness you look for in the end. Catapulting yourself into romantic entanglements that you know to be rather ill-advised is not sensible, and it would be better to wait before you committed yourself exclusively to any one person. It is the essence of your nature to serve the world at large and through doing so it is possible that you will attract money at some stage in your life.

Venus in Libra

Venus is very comfortable in Libra and bestows upon those people who have this planetary position a particular sort of kindness that is easy to recognise. This is a very good position for all sorts of friendships and also for romantic attachments that usually bring much joy into your life. Few individuals with Venus in Libra would avoid marriage and since you are capable of great depths of love, it is likely that you will find a contented personal life. You like to mix with people of integrity and intelligence but don't take kindly to scruffy surroundings or work that means getting your hands too dirty. Careful speculation, good business dealings and money through marriage all seem fairly likely.

Venus in Scorpio

You are quite open and tend to spend money quite freely, even on those occasions when you don't have very much. Although your intentions are always good, there are times when you get yourself in to the odd scrape and this can be particularly true when it comes to romance, which you may come to late or from a rather unexpected direction. Certainly you have the power to be happy and to make others contented on the way, but you find the odd stumbling block on your journey through life and it could seem that you have to work harder than those around you. As a result of this, you gain a much deeper understanding of the true value of personal happiness than many people ever do, and are likely to achieve true contentment in the end.

Venus in Sagittarius

You are lighthearted, cheerful and always able to see the funny side of any situation. These facts enhance your popularity, which is especially high with members of the opposite sex. You should never have to look too far to find romantic interest in your life, though it is just possible that you might be too willing to commit yourself before you are certain that the person in question is right for you. Part of the problem here extends to other areas of life too. The fact is that you like variety in everything and so can tire of situations that fail to offer it. All the same, if you choose wisely and learn to understand your restless side, then great happiness can be yours.

Venus in Capricorn

The most notable trait that comes from Venus in this position is that it makes you trustworthy and able to take on all sorts of responsibilities in life. People are instinctively fond of you and love you all the more because you are always ready to help those who are in any form of need. Social and business popularity can be yours and there is a magnetic quality to your nature that is particularly attractive in a romantic sense. Anyone who wants a partner for a lover, a spouse and a good friend too would almost certainly look in your direction. Constancy is the hallmark of your nature and unfaithfulness would go right against the grain. You might sometimes be a little too trusting.

Venus in Aquarius

This location of Venus offers a fondness for travel and a desire to try out something new at every possible opportunity. You are extremely easy to get along with and tend to have many friends from varied backgrounds, classes and inclinations. You like to live a distinct sort of life and gain a great deal from moving about, both in a career sense and with regard to your home. It is not out of the question that you could form a romantic attachment to someone who comes from far away or be attracted to a person of a distinctly artistic and original nature. What you cannot stand is jealousy, for you have friends of both sexes and would want to keep things that way.

Venus in Pisces

The first thing people tend to notice about you is your wonderful, warm smile. Being very charitable by nature you will do anything to help others, even if you don't know them well. Much of your life may be spent sorting out situations for other people, but it is very important to feel that you are living for yourself too. In the main, you remain cheerful, and tend to be quite attractive to members of the opposite sex. Where romantic attachments are concerned, you could be drawn to people who are significantly older or younger than yourself or to someone with a unique career or point of view. It might be best for you to avoid marrying whilst you are still very young.

THE ASTRAL DIARY

HOW THE DIAGRAMS WORK

Through the picture diagrams in the Astral Diary I want to help you to plot your year. With them you can see where the positive and negative aspects will be found in each month. To make the most of them, all you have to do is remember where and when!

Let me show you how they work ...

THE MONTH AT A GLANCE

Just as there are twelve separate zodiac signs, so astrologers believe that each sign has twelve separate aspects to life. Each of the twelve segments relates to a different personal aspect. I list them all every month so that their meanings are always clear.

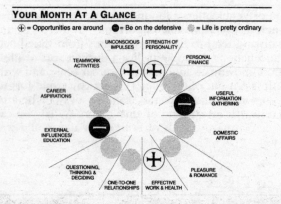

YOUR MONTH AT A GLANCE

⊕ = Opportunities are around ● = Be on the defensive ◌ = Life is pretty ordinary

UNCONSCIOUS IMPULSES
STRENGTH OF PERSONALITY
TEAMWORK ACTIVITIES
PERSONAL FINANCE
CAREER ASPIRATIONS
USEFUL INFORMATION GATHERING
EXTERNAL INFLUENCES/ EDUCATION
DOMESTIC AFFAIRS
QUESTIONING, THINKING & DECIDING
PLEASURE & ROMANCE
ONE-TO-ONE RELATIONSHIPS
EFFECTIVE WORK & HEALTH

I have designed this chart to show you how and when these twelve different aspects are being influenced throughout the year. When there is a shaded circle, nothing out of the ordinary is to be expected. However, when a circle turns white with a plus sign, the influence is positive. Where the circle is black with a minus sign, it is a negative.

YOUR ENERGY RHYTHM CHART

On the opposite page is a picture diagram in which I link your zodiac group to the rhythm of the Moon. In doing this I have calculated when you will be gaining strength from its influence and equally when you may be weakened by it.

If you think of yourself as being like the tides of the ocean then you may understand how your own energies must also rise and fall. And if you understand how it works and when it is working, then you can better organise your activities to achieve more and get things done more easily.

YOUR ENERGY RHYTHM CHART
At your best on 20th–21st

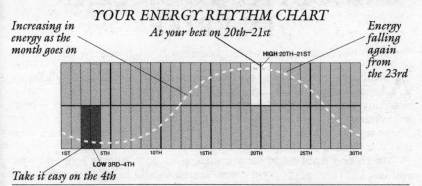

Increasing in energy as the month goes on

HIGH 20TH–21ST

Energy falling again from the 23rd

1ST 5TH 10TH 15TH 20TH 25TH 30TH

LOW 3RD–4TH

Take it easy on the 4th

MOVING PICTURE SCREEN
Love, money, career and vitality measured every week

The diagram at the end of each week is designed to be informative and fun. The arrows move up and down the scale to give you an idea of the strength of your opportunities in each area. If LOVE stands at plus 4, then get out and put yourself about because things are going your way in romance! The further down the arrow goes, the weaker the opportunities. Do note that the diagram is an overall view of your astrological aspects and therefore reflects a trend which may not concur with every day in that cycle.

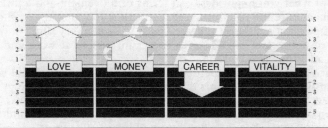

AND FINALLY:

am..

pm ....

The two lines that are left blank in each daily entry of the Astral Diary are for your own personal use. You may find them ideal for keeping a check on birthdays or appointments, though it could also be an idea to make notes from the astrological trends and diagrams a few weeks in advance. Some of the lines are marked with a key, which indicates the working of astrological cycles in your life. Look out for them each week as they are the best days to take action or make decisions. The daily text tells you which area of your life to focus on.

☿ = Mercury is retrograde on that day.

SCORPIO: YOUR YEAR IN BRIEF

As the new year begins, no amount of effort is wasted for Scorpio during January and February. It is really important for you to get the year started in the proper way and you won't be content with second best in anything you do. This attitude can lead to some frustrations but on the whole you should find this to be one of the most dynamic starts to a year that you have ever experienced.

March and April could see you having to slow down a little, only so you can see the wood for the trees. March should bring better financial prospects, or at least it might find you in the right frame of mind to deal with money, whilst April has a great deal going for it in a personal sense. People you see rarely are likely to reappear at this time and may bring with them some interesting surprises.

With April out of the way, May and June usher in the summer, a time of year that is likely to be a favourite for you. The better weather and longer days offer you more freedom and a greater sense of purpose than might have been the case earlier in the year. When it comes to personal popularity you are likely to be at your best at this time and June, in particular, may see you making some startling progress.

The high summer is likely to be an excellent time for you and offers much of what you might desire in terms of movement and a little more excitement entering your life. At the same time July and August show you to be capable of relaxation and you ought to be in a very family-motivated frame of mind. Get on side with successful people at work and follow their lead as much as you can.

Once September and October get underway you could feel yourself slowing down a little. It isn't that you fail to make any headway; merely that you are deciding to watch and wait in some situations. Family members could give you good reason to be proud of them and friends come up trumps when it really matters. You can afford to push your luck a little, especially during the last half of October.

The last two months of the year, November and December, might not seem to be particulary noteworthy in a day to day sense, but when you look at your tally of successes overall you should find that things are turning out rather well. You need to take some rest ahead of Christmas, and Christmas Day itself will need extra care in some respects, but in the main you finish the year satisfied with your efforts.

♍ January 2012

YOUR MONTH AT A GLANCE

⊕ = Opportunities are around   ⊖ = Be on the defensive   ● = Life is pretty ordinary

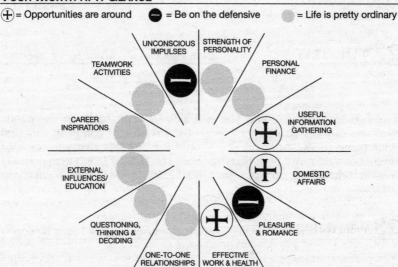

JANUARY HIGHS AND LOWS

Here I show you how the rhythms of the Moon will affect you this month. Like the tide, your energies and abilities will rise and fall with its pattern. When it is above the centre line, go for it, when it is below, you should be resting.

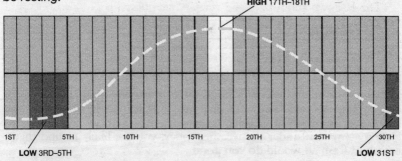

HIGH 17TH–18TH

1ST   5TH   10TH   15TH   20TH   25TH   30TH

LOW 3RD–5TH

LOW 31ST

41

26 MONDAY
Moon Age Day 1   Moon Sign Capricorn

am ....

pm ....

Trends suggest that for Boxing Day you should balance your options carefully and don't try to proceed until you know that you are likely to succeed. This is an especially important warning if you are working today. Don't expect everyone to be on your side at the moment but the people who really matter should support you fully.

27 TUESDAY
Moon Age Day 2   Moon Sign Capricorn

am ....

pm ....

The holidays continue and you will actively want to be in the public eye. You can get on very well in almost any sort of company. Practical skills come to the fore and you should use the fact that you are able to concentrate more now than has been the case of late. Certain family members may bring out your grumpy side, so stay away from them if you can.

28 WEDNESDAY
Moon Age Day 3   Moon Sign Aquarius

am ....

pm ....

It looks as though you will soon be entering a period during which it will be easy to bring others round to your particular point of view. Almost anyone is susceptible to your charms right now so use that fact to advance your plans. Some people recognise an air of mystery about you and this should be encouraged.

29 THURSDAY
Moon Age Day 4   Moon Sign Aquarius

am ....

pm ....

Venus moves on and you may be prone to especially high ideals or even certain illusions regarding your own life. Talk to people who are in the know and be prepared to learn from what they have to say. If you are feeling somewhat under the weather today, you are likely to find that a breath of fresh air would do you good.

30 FRIDAY
Moon Age Day 5   Moon Sign Pisces

am ....

pm..

Socially speaking you need to keep your options open. Not everything is going to work out entirely as you might wish and a little extra patience could be required. Some travel is possible, so maybe you are going to spend New Year away from home. Short journeys seem best, but any sort of change might appeal.

31 SATURDAY
Moon Age Day 6   Moon Sign Pisces

am ....

pm..

It's time for the final fling before you get yourself back into gear to face a brand new year. Today should be all about clearing up 2011 and looking towards what lies ahead of you. Friends should be filled with bright ideas but you are most likely to be spending the evening in the company of the person who is most special to you.

1 SUNDAY
Moon Age Day 7   Moon Sign Aries

am ....

pm..

Although your intuition works well as a rule, people are anything but easy to understand as this New Year begins. There is not much that you can take for granted when it comes to appreciating what makes others tick today, which is why you should choose to ask a few pertinent questions.

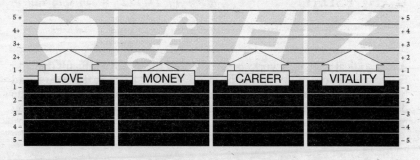

2 MONDAY
Moon Age Day 8   Moon Sign Aries

am ....

pm...

You need to keep a careful eye on how much you are spending. Luxury goods are allowed, of course, but probably not very often. What counts most right now is that you read the small print on any agreement carefully, or better still leave deals or documents until later. Financial complexity could be surrounding you at this time.

3 TUESDAY
Moon Age Day 9   Moon Sign Taurus

am ....

pm...

There may be the odd challenge to deal with today, perhaps as a result of the fact that you can't agree with everyone. Some people appear determined to make themselves difficult. As a rule, you would simply shrug your shoulders and accept the situation. If you are tempted to challenge people today, perhaps you could give it a second thought.

4 WEDNESDAY
Moon Age Day 10   Moon Sign Taurus

am ....

pm...

Things are quieter today and tomorrow and there appears to be very little you can do about this situation. You can thank the lunar low for the present state of affairs and should simply jog along as best you can and ride out the trend. There may be some light relief coming from the comical behaviour of family members.

5 THURSDAY
Moon Age Day 11   Moon Sign Taurus

am ....

pm...

A methodical approach works best today and this is not a difficult demand for your zodiac sign. What might go against the grain is that you could have to go over some jobs that you thought were finished. Despite the desire to make fresh starts, you need to finish certain tasks before you push on with others.

6 FRIDAY
Moon Age Day 12   Moon Sign Gemini

am ....

pm..

Your intuition is strong today and some unusual planetary influences make it more than likely that you will be happy to back your hunches. If you feel you are exuding charm, don't be surprised if you find you are getting plenty of attention coming back in your direction.

7 SATURDAY
Moon Age Day 13   Moon Sign Gemini

am ....

pm..

If you get the opportunity, this would be a good day to assert yourself in a professional sense. Personal attachments could prove to be just a little difficult, not least of all because others are failing to behave in a way you might expect. You will need to be psychic to know what makes your partner tick now so tread cautiously!

8 SUNDAY
Moon Age Day 14   Moon Sign Cancer

am ....

pm..

The planets are certainly smiling on Scorpio the social animal right now so you should be making sure your diary is full because the possibilities are endless. You can afford to push your luck a little and should expect to make gains. Now is a period for putting new initiatives to the test and for getting on extremely well in life generally.

9 MONDAY
Moon Age Day 15   Moon Sign Cancer

am ....

pm ....

If you are a Scorpian who is looking for work, you really should be keeping your eyes open right now. Money matters should be less complicated for you than of late. Today, you may have the need to get an emotional issue out of the way before you find yourself in a position to do whatever it is that you really want to do.

10 TUESDAY
Moon Age Day 16   Moon Sign Cancer

am ....

pm ....

You should be thinking quickly and clearly and feeling generally optimistic about life. The advice of other people is important but you also need to rely on your own instincts now. You could be making certain life choices now but these are not likely to prove a problem under such positive trends.

11 WEDNESDAY
Moon Age Day 17   Moon Sign Leo

am ....

pm ....

If you have one eye on the future, be careful not to paint too gloomy a picture of the potential outcome. You should be good at maintaining the gains that have been so apparent in your life over the last few days and this is likely to be a generally carefree and happy period.

12 THURSDAY
Moon Age Day 18   Moon Sign Leo

am ....

pm ....

Although you would be best to commit yourself to practical matters in the morning, by the time the afternoon wears on you start to look at your social calendar for the next few days. If you feel yourself to be subject to any sort of threat, particularly related to your work, it is likely to awaken your fighting instincts – don't overdo it.

13 FRIDAY
Moon Age Day 19   Moon Sign Virgo

am ....

pm ....

Be careful that you don't upset others by being too determined to get your own way. It is vitally important to explain yourself around now and your powers of communication are good enough to allow this. All the same, you may feel an increasing need for independence that will be difficult to keep under wraps.

14 SATURDAY
Moon Age Day 20   Moon Sign Virgo

am ....

pm ....

There is a fine line between doing what suits you and upsetting other people because they don't understand and this is what you have to negotiate. It won't be easy to be entirely truthful at present, but you owe it to the ones you care about at least to try. Scorpio can be extremely intense and that is obvious for most of you today.

15 SUNDAY
Moon Age Day 21   Moon Sign Libra

am ....

pm ....

In discussions, you may prove that you are able to mix tact and truthfulness, which is not a skill possessed by all zodiac signs. Relatives need your attentive ear and unique attitude now. At best, you can be very innovative today so you should use that to support people who are looking at old tasks in new ways.

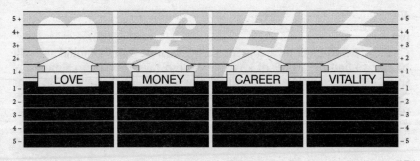

16 MONDAY
Moon Age Day 22   Moon Sign Libra

am ....

pm...

You may succeed particularly well in partnerships at this time and might find that you are getting on especially well with people who meant little to you in the past. If you make good use of this spirit of compromise and flexibility, you should open up all sorts of new avenues.

17 TUESDAY
Moon Age Day 23   Moon Sign Scorpio

am ....

pm...

There is great scope for using your intuition and your practical skills while the lunar high is present. Although someone is more or less bound to feel left out, it is imperative that you follow your own mind, no matter where it takes you. The slower types will simply have to catch up when they can, whilst you zoom ahead.

18 WEDNESDAY
Moon Age Day 24   Moon Sign Scorpio

am ....

pm...

You should be pleased to monitor the fact that your mental and physical strengths are reaching a definite peak. Make the most of positive situations and enhance your efforts by turning on all the charm that your sign of Scorpio presently allows. Utilise the fact that your diplomatic skills are now much better than usual.

19 THURSDAY
Moon Age Day 25   Moon Sign Sagittarius

am ....

pm...

Chances are you will be in a particularly romantic frame of mind and will be able to find the words of love that are most appropriate to almost any situation. Take advantage of helpful new influences that appear in your professional life. These offer incentives that didn't show up even a few days ago.

20 FRIDAY   *Moon Age Day 26   Moon Sign Sagittarius*

am...

pm...

Highlight the romantic matters in your life today and respond positively to any genuine compliments that come your way. This isn't the best time to stick to mundane issues. Instead, busy yourself with exciting projects and the possibilities that lie ahead in both a personal and a professional sense.

21 SATURDAY   *Moon Age Day 27   Moon Sign Capricorn*

am...

pm...

There's a suggestion that you'll encounter a few disappointments in your love life. You are usually willing to do whatever you can to fulfil the needs and wants of your partner, but the demands that are made of you today could seem excessive. The best way to overcome this is to think and look towards the longer term.

22 SUNDAY   *Moon Age Day 28   Moon Sign Capricorn*

am...

pm...

There is much that is casual about today, but this merely hides some essential truths. You ought to be able to deal quite positively with an issue from the past that has been hanging over you for some time. This will lead to a lessening of anxiety, much of which did not need to be there in the first place.

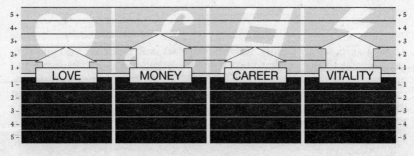

23 MONDAY
Moon Age Day 0   Moon Sign Capricorn

am ....

pm...

This should be a positive sort of day, filled with social and personal possibilities and replete with 'happenings' that seem designed to cheer you. Tap into the fact that others can boost your ego at present, which is no bad thing for someone who is born under a water sign, as you are, and is not always as confident as they could be.

24 TUESDAY
Moon Age Day 1   Moon Sign Aquarius

am ....

pm...

If you find that you are spending much of your time doing things for other people and offering a listening ear or a shoulder to cry on, do make sure you don't forget your own needs too. The sympathy you show towards others is strong at the best of times, but much more so today.

25 WEDNESDAY
Moon Age Day 2   Moon Sign Aquarius

am ....

pm...

Although some jobs could bore you a little, you should undertake them with a good will and plenty of humour. Take action on matters related to getting ahead, as ambitious matters of all kinds are assisted by the some good planetary trends. When you decide on a particular course of action, stick to it and see it through to the end.

26 THURSDAY
Moon Age Day 3   Moon Sign Pisces

am ....

pm...

Today has its strong points. Relationships are well aspected, and you may have reason to notice that your romantic attachments are stronger and promise to be more enduring than expected. When it comes to ordinary, everyday friendship, look to the people around you, who will be willing to show just how much you mean to them.

27 FRIDAY
Moon Age Day 4   Moon Sign Pisces

am..

pm..

If you get the mundane tasks out of the way early in the day, you'll have more time to do what you really want to do. That should be going out and meeting people, whatever the context. Socially speaking, you should really be turning up the heat and making sure you have plenty of things to do and places to go.

28 SATURDAY
Moon Age Day 5   Moon Sign Aries

am..

pm..

A methodical approach works best today and Scorpio is good at that. However, you might have to redo something you thought was finished, which won't please you but the less fuss you make, the sooner it will be out of the way. You do need to finish what you have started before you move on.

29 SUNDAY
Moon Age Day 6   Moon Sign Aries

am..

pm..

There's some luck shining on you today so maybe you could cautiously back your hunches. The next day or two probably won't be too exciting so enjoy yourself this evening. Money-making endeavours are well highlighted so you could discover that you have the knack of getting things right.

30 MONDAY
Moon Age Day 7   Moon Sign Aries

am ....

pm...

The sense of nostalgia is palpable today, combined with a strong focus on the family, making this the perfect day for a family gathering. Although you are unlikely to be travelling yourself, you will be pleased to have as many people you love as possible surrounding you.

31 TUESDAY
Moon Age Day 8   Moon Sign Taurus

am ....

pm...

Domestic issues may crowd in on you, just at the time when you could do with some relaxation. Leave certain situations on the back burner if you can force yourself to do so. There are people around who will help you, but can you really be bothered to seek them out at the moment?

1 WEDNESDAY
Moon Age Day 9   Moon Sign Taurus

am ....

pm...

It is towards your career that your mind is apt to turn now. Conflict with someone you know well can be avoided if you simply refuse to become involved, whilst the relationship you have with your partner is going from strength to strength. A little bad news later probably turns out to be rather far-fetched.

2 THURSDAY
Moon Age Day 10   Moon Sign Gemini

am ....

pm...

Keep a sense of proportion and don't allow yourself to be fazed by the slightly mystifying behaviour of other people. You will be quite anxious to stick up for yourself at this time. Where social arrangements are concerned, you need to be aware that difficulties could arise, probably regarding arrangements.

3 FRIDAY
Moon Age Day 11   Moon Sign Gemini

am ....

pm..

You can expect a busy day, but one that works mainly in your favour. If there appears to be nothing ahead but work and worry, you really are not looking at the positive side of life as much as you should. Your power to attract the better things in life certainly seems to be improving now.

4 SATURDAY
Moon Age Day 12   Moon Sign Gemini

am ....

pm..

You should be feeling confident now – perhaps a little too confident for your own good! Scorpio isn't too good at humility at the best of times, and you need to be careful that it doesn't desert you entirely. There is a tendency towards a know-it-all attitude on your part today that you need to work against.

5 SUNDAY
Moon Age Day 13   Moon Sign Cancer

am ....

pm..

You have plenty of enthusiasm and a definite desire to get on well in life. Your present driving force is unlikely to abandon you in the short term, so you can take a few chances. Right now certain people, and especially authority figures, are more than willing to offer you some help along the path towards your own success.

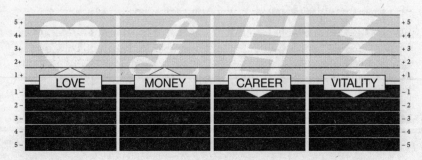

February 2012

YOUR MONTH AT A GLANCE

⊕ = Opportunities are around   ⊖ = Be on the defensive   ⬤ = Life is pretty ordinary

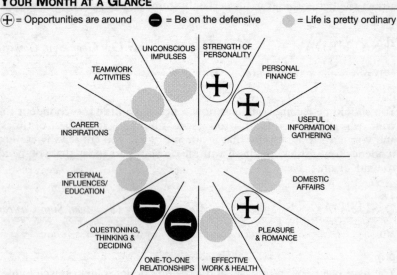

UNCONSCIOUS IMPULSES

STRENGTH OF PERSONALITY

TEAMWORK ACTIVITIES

PERSONAL FINANCE

CAREER INSPIRATIONS

USEFUL INFORMATION GATHERING

EXTERNAL INFLUENCES/ EDUCATION

DOMESTIC AFFAIRS

QUESTIONING, THINKING & DECIDING

PLEASURE & ROMANCE

ONE-TO-ONE RELATIONSHIPS

EFFECTIVE WORK & HEALTH

FEBRUARY HIGHS AND LOWS

Here I show you how the rhythms of the Moon will affect you this month. Like the tide, your energies and abilities will rise and fall with its pattern. When it is above the centre line, go for it, when it is below, you should be resting.

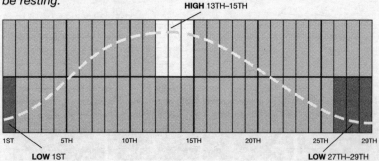

HIGH 13TH–15TH

1ST   5TH   10TH   15TH   20TH   25TH   29TH

LOW 1ST   LOW 27TH–29TH

6 MONDAY
Moon Age Day 14   Moon Sign Cancer

am...

pm...

Confidence still isn't lacking and as the week wears on it becomes obvious that you can steer yourself towards one or two triumphs. Although you are happy to take time off from certain obligations, in the main you should be choosing your own path today and showing certainty in what you are doing.

7 TUESDAY
Moon Age Day 15   Moon Sign Leo

am...

pm...

You could be on the receiving end of some especially good news and it would certainly not be a bad time to make some changes in your life, maybe associated in some way with your house and home. You may be aware of other people having a strong influence over you at present, especially at work.

8 WEDNESDAY
Moon Age Day 16   Moon Sign Leo

am...

pm...

Watch out for financial opportunities and be prepared to invest a little now in order to make substantial gains later. Professionally speaking, if you put in plenty of effort you should be able to advance your career. Some longer-term planning you have undertaken could now be beginning to pay dividends.

9 THURSDAY
Moon Age Day 17   Moon Sign Virgo

am...

pm...

Entertainment is something you look out for and when it comes to keeping your friends occupied you appear to be especially proficient at present. You should be capitalising on positive social trends and making the most of out-of-work hours. You will need to work hard to interpret the attitude of a friend.

10 FRIDAY

Moon Age Day 18   Moon Sign Virgo

am ....

pm ....

Unless you are truly the intrepid Scorpio type, you are likely to find toasting your toes in front of a warming fire much more appealing now than fresh air and exercise. This would also be a good time to focus on relationships as they can offer some rich rewards if you put in the effort.

11 SATURDAY

Moon Age Day 19   Moon Sign Libra

am ....

pm ....

Scorpians who are at home today will probably still choose to find something new and exciting to do. Those who are at work can expect colleagues to be deferential and might even hear about possible advancement. In almost every sense, but especially professionally, you should be maximising this winning streak.

12 SUNDAY

Moon Age Day 20   Moon Sign Libra

am ....

pm ....

Not everything about today is easy, though you will relish some of the challenges that you face. You might suspect others of not being totally honest in their dealings with you at present. Chances are that you will be correct in your assumptions, though it will give you little pleasure to realise this fact.

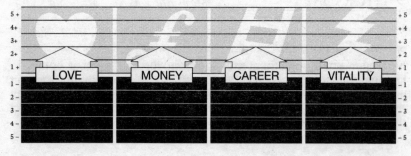

13 MONDAY
Moon Age Day 21   Moon Sign Scorpio

am ....

pm ....

Along comes the lunar high and a time to really shine in all public situations. Although you can be naturally shy on some occasions, this doesn't turn out to be the case at all now. Personal projects are very much to the fore and you should focus on what you most want to achieve as you are likely to get things just right.

14 TUESDAY
Moon Age Day 22   Moon Sign Scorpio

am ....

pm ....

This is probably the best day of the month to steam ahead at full speed. The lunar high offers all sorts of incentives, not least of all a silver tongue and the ability to lift the veil, ever so slightly, on that mysterious nature of yours. There's no doubt that you appear to be particularly attractive now.

15 WEDNESDAY
Moon Age Day 23   Moon Sign Scorpio

am ....

pm ....

Now the Moon is firmly settled in your zodiac sign and this is a time for having fun. You can be reassured that most of your aims and objectives are reasonable and if you apply your present confidence, you should be able to achieve them. With a higher degree of good luck coming your way, you can afford limited speculation during today.

16 THURSDAY
Moon Age Day 24   Moon Sign Sagittarius

am ....

pm ....

Try hard today because promotion could be on the cards and you won't want to pass up the chance. For those of you who are simply determined to relax at this stage of the week, there could be some luxury in store. All in all, this is a time for emphasising your practical skills and for showing anyone who doubts you that you know what you are doing.

17 FRIDAY
Moon Age Day 25   Moon Sign Sagittarius

am...

pm...

In all practical matters, you must exercise a great deal of care. It is too easy at present to push yourself harder than you intended, which could lead to a degree of fatigue. Whilst your home and family life looks very settled at present, you are likely to be having a more uneven time at work.

18 SATURDAY
Moon Age Day 26   Moon Sign Capricorn

am...

pm...

It is true that you may have to force someone to do something they are not looking forward to, but this is a minor issue, bearing in mind your amazing ability to talk people round to your particular point of view. Life is on a roll now and the weekend could prove to be especially interesting.

19 SUNDAY
Moon Age Day 27   Moon Sign Capricorn

am...

pm...

Don't be in the least surprised if people are saying pleasant things to you today – they mean it. The thirst for fresh fields and pastures new is especially strong so you may want to plan a trip. Although you might be embarking on a very busy time in a practical sense, try to find time for some variety.

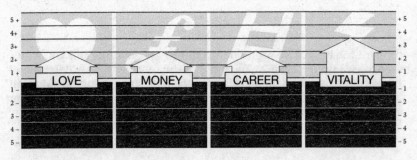

20 MONDAY
Moon Age Day 28   Moon Sign Aquarius

am ....

pm ....

Today ought to be favourable for progress in one specific direction. This is not a time to try to do a thousand different jobs at once. Focus your mind on a particular objective and almost anything becomes possible. It may be that not everything turns out exactly as you planned but sometimes that's for the best.

21 TUESDAY
Moon Age Day 29   Moon Sign Aquarius

am ....

pm ....

There are individuals around who can be extremely useful to you, but it's a two-way street so look for contacts with whom you can have a mutually beneficial dialogue. You are probably in for a busy day, but since it is also generally successful, the time passes quickly and happily. Career progress is quite easy to achieve.

22 WEDNESDAY
Moon Age Day 0   Moon Sign Pisces

am ....

pm ....

A few unexpected setbacks are likely now, thanks to a fairly temporary association of planets. At the very worst, this is a small storm you can ride quite successfully. However, it is important to look ahead and to use your intuition. What it tells you about the trustworthy nature of others is very important.

23 THURSDAY
Moon Age Day 1   Moon Sign Pisces

am ....

pm ....

Reaching out to a good friend who is having problems at present would be a wonderful gesture. Love life and romantic interests are likely to go your way at this time. With friends and relatives lending a hand, you have more time to think about those very personal contacts that mean the most to you.

24 FRIDAY

Moon Age Day 2   Moon Sign Pisces

am...

pm...

Look out for some hopeful news that could enliven things no end. You are in the mood for excitement and can put yourself out to make sure that others have a good time as well. You are feeling confident enough to make some changes in one way or another, specifically with regard to travel.

25 SATURDAY

Moon Age Day 3   Moon Sign Aries

am...

pm...

You may find you need to be diplomatic but firm, and most people will respect you for that. This is not a good time to be involved in conflict with colleagues or friends. You are going to get on much better if you create a harmonious atmosphere, though you shouldn't have to subjugate your own wishes entirely.

26 SUNDAY

Moon Age Day 4   Moon Sign Aries

am...

pm...

This may not be a day for too many adventures, but small ones can be fun. There are some very grateful people around now, perhaps because of things you have done for them recently. They are likely to show their gratitude in a number of different ways, all of which should please you.

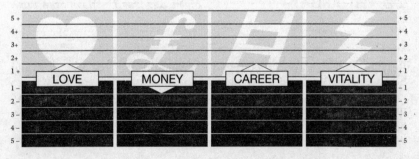

27 MONDAY
Moon Age Day 5   Moon Sign Taurus

am ....

pm ....

You may prefer to avoid too much in the way of action today. The fact is that you are in a fairly low-key frame of mind and this is mainly due to the lunar low, which settles on you at present. This allows you time to think and to lay down plans for later, which you should appreciate long-term.

28 TUESDAY
Moon Age Day 6   Moon Sign Taurus

am ....

pm ....

Once again, you need to take life steadily and to allow others to do some of the running around. If family members in particular are not keen to let you have a break, remind them of all you do on their behalf. You engender a good deal of love in others, so those close to you should be willing to spoil you now.

29 WEDNESDAY
Moon Age Day 7   Moon Sign Taurus

am ....

pm ....

Although the domestic scene is the one you enjoy the most, things that are happening at home right now might not please you very much. Socialising with friends is an option, but you won't get too far by trying to sort out people who seem determined to be awkward. Allow them time to calm down and think things through.

1 THURSDAY
Moon Age Day 8   Moon Sign Gemini

am ....

pm ....

For the first time this year, it could occur to you that spring is just around the corner, a state of affairs that should cheer you up no end. Romantically and personally, it appears that you have opportunities for the taking. Professional issues will find you making the best of yourself today, as a new month begins.

2 FRIDAY
Moon Age Day 9   Moon Sign Gemini

am ....

pm..

Don't get so wrapped up in your own opinions today that you fail to notice what your nearest and dearest are trying to say to you. It is unlikely that this trend relates to practical matters, more to subjects related to home and family. As is often the case, this is the sphere of life that concerns you the most.

3 SATURDAY
Moon Age Day 10   Moon Sign Cancer

am ....

pm..

Keep it simple, that's the key for today. Anything major will respond better to the trends of next week so it's best to delay major decisions. You are in an optimistic frame of mind so use that to encourage and even amuse many of the people you come across today. This may not be a good time for breaking big news.

4 SUNDAY
Moon Age Day 11   Moon Sign Cancer

am ....

pm..

If old topics have arisen, you should be able to start thinking about them in a very new way. This may be because you are willing to follow the line of least resistance and tap into the spirit of harmony that exists today. This being the case, you could enhance your popularity and people will forget any recent hiccups.

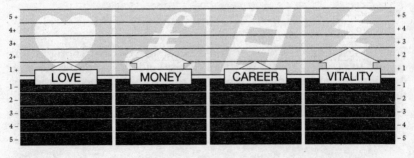

March

2012

YOUR MONTH AT A GLANCE

⊕ = Opportunities are around   ⊖ = Be on the defensive   ⬤ = Life is pretty ordinary

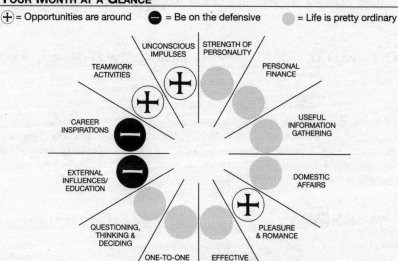

- UNCONSCIOUS IMPULSES
- STRENGTH OF PERSONALITY
- TEAMWORK ACTIVITIES
- PERSONAL FINANCE
- CAREER INSPIRATIONS
- USEFUL INFORMATION GATHERING
- EXTERNAL INFLUENCES/ EDUCATION
- DOMESTIC AFFAIRS
- QUESTIONING, THINKING & DECIDING
- PLEASURE & ROMANCE
- ONE-TO-ONE RELATIONSHIPS
- EFFECTIVE WORK & HEALTH

MARCH HIGHS AND LOWS

Here I show you how the rhythms of the Moon will affect you this month. Like the tide, your energies and abilities will rise and fall with its pattern. When it is above the centre line, go for it, when it is below, you should be resting.

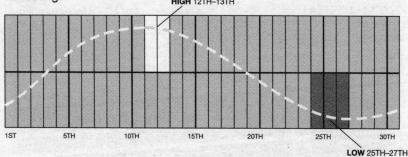

HIGH 12TH–13TH

1ST   5TH   10TH   15TH   20TH   25TH   30TH

LOW 25TH–27TH

63

5 MONDAY
Moon Age Day 12   Moon Sign Leo

am ....

pm ....

Anything that requires convincing others should wait until later in the week. Keep it uncomplicated, at least for the next few days. Endless debates that prove nothing and are a waste of your time at the moment. Instead of being involved in them, it would be best for you to simply address issues that are not contentious.

6 TUESDAY
Moon Age Day 13   Moon Sign Leo

am ....

pm ....

In a social sense you are should be making sure you mix with a variety of people, and you should be active on the romantic front too. You can definitely gain from a hands-on approach to most aspects of life today. Getting stuck in will get you noticed, which in turn can lead to better prospects further down the line.

7 WEDNESDAY
Moon Age Day 14   Moon Sign Leo

am ....

pm ....

You should be getting on well with everyone and it is very unlikely that you will fail to see eye to eye with those around you. You exhibit the most charming side of your harmonious zodiac sign when you are feeling in such a co-operative frame of mind. From the point of view of getting practical things done, today should be ideal.

8 THURSDAY
Moon Age Day 15   Moon Sign Virgo

am ....

pm ....

Socially speaking you are on good form generally but may take the greatest pleasure from romantic attachments. Communication issues are also likely to be good today, making for a time when you find it easy to explain what you want, and can also interpret accurately what other people are trying to say to you.

9 FRIDAY

Moon Age Day 16   Moon Sign Virgo

am ....

pm ....

All of a sudden, nostalgia rules in practically everything, and you would probably enjoy reading a classic book or watching an old movie now. It is amazing today how much your mind goes back to times and situations in the past. If you take the trouble to work out where you went wrong before, you can gain by doing things differently this time.

10 SATURDAY

Moon Age Day 17   Moon Sign Libra

am ....

pm ....

There is now a strong emphasis on leisure and pleasure pursuits, so make sure you are active on the social front. To maximise your opportunities, you should make the choices on what to do; other people should be happy to come along for the ride. Some Scorpians will have the summer in view already but it's too early to focus on holidays just yet.

11 SUNDAY

Moon Age Day 18   Moon Sign Libra

am ....

pm ....

You should find that your friends are expressing more than their usual warmth to you, and they could have some fascinating things to tell you. If you are willing to put effort into your relationships, you are likely to get much more back. Certainly this is the case when you co-operate because the sum of the parts can be greater than its components right now.

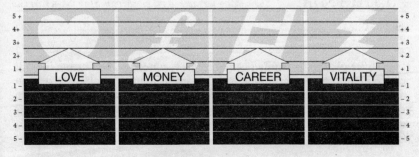

12 MONDAY ☿ *Moon Age Day 19 Moon Sign Scorpio*

am ....

pm...

Thanks to the lunar high, you should be able to achieve many things with less trouble than you anticipated, so good progress should be possible. People are likely to notice that you have great vitality and popularity. Be certain of your own capabilities and that will give you the confidence to persuade any doubters around you.

13 TUESDAY ☿ *Moon Age Day 20 Moon Sign Scorpio*

am ....

pm...

Now the lunar high offers you all the incentive and drive that you could possibly wish for. This ought to be an excellent time for getting out and about, or for enlisting the support of friends when it comes to plans you have been hatching for a while. Very little has changed, and yet almost everything feels different.

14 WEDNESDAY ☿ *Moon Age Day 21 Moon Sign Sagittarius*

am ....

pm...

If anything is worrying you today, it is important to speak to the people concerned. What you definitely don't need under current trends is to allow any sort of situation to get out of hand. There could be too much emotional tension in your life right now and this is something that you need to work against.

15 THURSDAY ☿ *Moon Age Day 22 Moon Sign Sagittarius*

am ....

pm...

If you have planned a family get-together, you need to be flexible in your arrangements. Not everything today is going to turn out quite as you would have anticipated but that doesn't mean cancelling anything. Keep your eyes and ears open because there is likely to be some important news coming your way.

16 FRIDAY
☿ *Moon Age Day 23* *Moon Sign Capricorn*

am ....

pm ....

When it comes to getting what you want, you can be second to none now and show a great ability to persuade others that your point of view is the right one. Don't be too quick to jump to conclusions in matters relating to love. You should try to make use of some pretty subtle tactics at present.

17 SATURDAY
☿ *Moon Age Day 24* *Moon Sign Capricorn*

am ....

pm ....

Good friends you haven't seen for some time make a return visit to your life and even general gossip is of specific interest to you right now. Plan a journey today, even if it won't take place for months. Friendship and group encounters take on a good feel so seek out ventures involving co-operation.

18 SUNDAY
☿ *Moon Age Day 25* *Moon Sign Capricorn*

am ....

pm ....

There is no doubt you are at your very best now when you socialise with trusted friends or relatives. A quieter day can be expected because some planetary trends are steadier than previously. You will need to check and recheck certain matters before you commit yourself and there could be a slight feeling of lethargy.

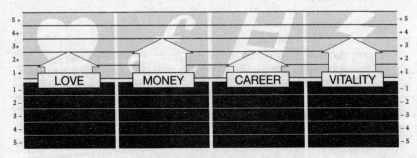

19 MONDAY ☿ *Moon Age Day 26   Moon Sign Aquarius*

am...

pm...

You might try the odd cautious gamble now, since general good luck is with you. A free and easy approach goes a long way at the beginning of this week. Although you may feel that you are being asked to do more than you consider to be your remit, you can turn that to a positive and impress some influential people on the way.

20 TUESDAY ☿ *Moon Age Day 27   Moon Sign Aquarius*

am...

pm...

When it comes to major decisions that have a bearing on the longer-term aspects of life, you could do worse than to seek the help and support of friends who know you very well. It would be far better to think matters through carefully now, rather than rushing at stopgap measures..

21 WEDNESDAY ☿ *Moon Age Day 28   Moon Sign Pisces*

am...

pm...

You might have trouble getting through to people who think about life very differently from the way you do. But you also need to accept that those around you have the right to be the way they naturally are, even if you disagree. You can try to assert your ideas at home, perhaps with some success, but this is not so easy in the wider world.

22 THURSDAY ☿ *Moon Age Day 0   Moon Sign Pisces*

am...

pm...

You could do worse today than to find yourself somewhere new and unusual to go. There are plenty of possibilities and the more you think about it, the greater are your options. The only slight problem is that you will try to do everything at the same time, a course of action that is very likely to lead to regular failures and some disappointment.

23 FRIDAY ☿ *Moon Age Day 1   Moon Sign Aries*

am ....

pm ....

The end of the working week will offer you the chance to plan ahead towards a weekend that can offer significant rewards. Romance could well be highlighted by this evening. A positive focus on career developments helps to take your mind off slightly negative trends in other directions.

24 SATURDAY ☿ *Moon Age Day 2   Moon Sign Aries*

am ....

pm ....

This is an ideal time for shopping, travelling, going out with friends and doing a host of other things that are right up your street. In personal relationships, you value give and take and will be fun to have around under most circumstances. Getting a great deal done is par for the course this Saturday.

25 SUNDAY ☿ *Moon Age Day 3   Moon Sign Taurus*

am ....

pm ....

You show yourself to be a good listener today, which is a positive way to use the lunar low period. Make time to hear exactly what other people are saying and to do what you can to help them to sort out their problems. Most of the people you meet retain a deep confidence in you so always make sure you respect their secrets.

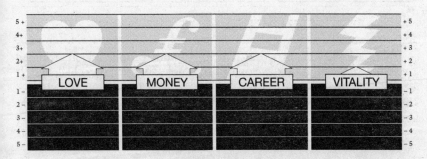

26 MONDAY ☿ *Moon Age Day 4   Moon Sign Taurus*

am ....

pm..

In emotional attachments, there are likely to be a few stresses at the moment. The best way to avoid these is to keep things light and open. Deep and meaningful conversations are probably not the best way to move forward at present. There could be slightly more cash about today than you had been expecting.

27 TUESDAY ☿ *Moon Age Day 5   Moon Sign Taurus*

am ....

pm..

You may not have a massive bearing on society today, even at a local level, but every little helps. Concern for others is always a part of what you are but rarely more so than seems to be the case now. Be attentive and you may hear some useful things, while you should be prepared to accept help when it is offered.

28 WEDNESDAY ☿ *Moon Age Day 6   Moon Sign Gemini*

am ....

pm..

Keep your eye on whatever target you have set yourself and don't be willing to keep doing something you know is beneath your abilities. Others will help you out, but most likely only if you ask. There is a genuine possibility that you can move up the professional ladder at some stage soon.

29 THURSDAY ☿ *Moon Age Day 7   Moon Sign Gemini*

am ....

pm..

If there are disputes at work, it is up to you to pour oil on troubled waters. Even taking on jobs you dislike is not too much of a challenge. It is true that the ups and downs of everyday life continue but you are in a good position to deal with both, rationally and with great common sense.

30 FRIDAY ☿ *Moon Age Day 8   Moon Sign Cancer*

am ....

pm..

When you have set your mind on a particular course of action, don't take no for an answer. Now there is extra confidence and happiness showing up in your social life. New friends are likely to appear around now and they bring with them the chance to look at old issues in new ways.

31 SATURDAY ☿ *Moon Age Day 9   Moon Sign Cancer*

am ....

pm..

You could need some special help today in order to get you out of a jam, though it is one that owes nothing to your own decisions or past actions. If you explain yourself to the right people, there is every reason to believe they can reverse difficult situations. Remaining positive will the best way to make sure things turn out well.

1 SUNDAY ☿ *Moon Age Day 10   Moon Sign Cancer*

am ....

pm..

Someone is filled with admiration regarding the way you have dealt with a specific issue and it looks as though you are going to be number one in their books. Social matters and teamwork situations are where your most rewarding moments arise once the new working week gets started.

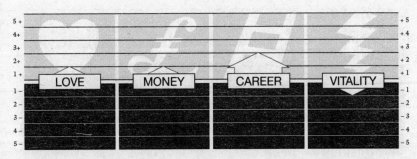

April

2012

Your Month at a Glance

⊕ = Opportunities are around   ⊖ = Be on the defensive   ⬤ = Life is pretty ordinary

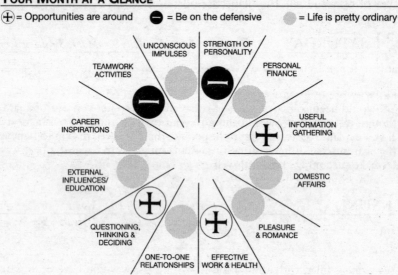

UNCONSCIOUS IMPULSES

STRENGTH OF PERSONALITY

TEAMWORK ACTIVITIES

PERSONAL FINANCE

CAREER INSPIRATIONS

USEFUL INFORMATION GATHERING

EXTERNAL INFLUENCES/ EDUCATION

DOMESTIC AFFAIRS

QUESTIONING, THINKING & DECIDING

PLEASURE & ROMANCE

ONE-TO-ONE RELATIONSHIPS

EFFECTIVE WORK & HEALTH

April Highs and Lows

Here I show you how the rhythms of the Moon will affect you this month. Like the tide, your energies and abilities will rise and fall with its pattern. When it is above the centre line, go for it, when it is below, you should be resting.

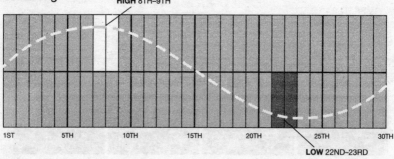

HIGH 8TH–9TH

1ST   5TH   10TH   15TH   20TH   25TH   30TH

LOW 22ND–23RD

2 MONDAY ☿ *Moon Age Day 11 Moon Sign Leo*

am ....

pm...

Don't worry about the somewhat offhand attitude of a specific friend today. They are going through a rather hard time and could be inclined to lash out at those they care for the most. Looking at life through the eyes of other people has never been easier and this can prove to be a tremendous gift.

3 TUESDAY ☿ *Moon Age Day 12 Moon Sign Leo*

am ....

pm...

A quite voluble and emotionally inspired Scorpio is something the world doesn't see every day, so you are bound to receive a good deal of attention at this time. The new month has barely started and you will want to get on with making it a positive one just as soon as you can. Friends should be a great help at all stages this week.

4 WEDNESDAY ☿ *Moon Age Day 13 Moon Sign Virgo*

am ....

pm...

You may have an idea of what you would like to do socially and not be able to make it happen, but that doesn't mean you shouldn't try. In fact, whatever you decide to do is likely to be enjoyable. Scorpio can be a very understated sign, which is why you look so powerful when you do turn up the volume. Prepare to be noticed.

5 THURSDAY *Moon Age Day 14 Moon Sign Virgo*

am ....

pm...

There are likely to be messages coming along from people you don't see very often. Partnerships improve and it doesn't matter if these are of a professional or a personal nature. Use a powerful mixture of intuition and practical common sense to lead you forward, and enlist the support of those around you.

6 FRIDAY

Moon Age Day 15   Moon Sign Libra

am ....

pm ....

Seek out those who are in the know and if you are deciding on some new sort of hobby, make sure everything is in place before you get started. It's vital to do so. A helping hand can be quite important to you and offers you the chance to get ahead in something you didn't really think you were good at.

7 SATURDAY

Moon Age Day 16   Moon Sign Libra

am ....

pm ....

At work you could be frustrated by rules and regulations. However, whenever you are working amongst groups around this time, your performance is likely to outshine your colleagues. It isn't that you leap to the front and show a determination to be the best of the bunch but rather you impress with your great co-operation and team spirit.

8 SUNDAY

Moon Age Day 17   Moon Sign Scorpio

am ....

pm ....

Your personal influence has never been stronger this month than it proves to be right now. You have energy to spare and it should seem as though all the things you have been looking for manage to come together at the same time. Try to avoid too much work because it is clear you need space to breathe.

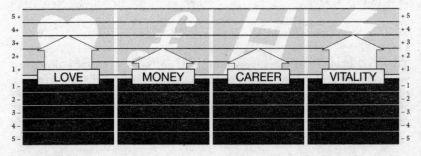

9 MONDAY

Moon Age Day 18   Moon Sign Scorpio

am ....

pm...

Treat today as the beginning of a brighter and better phase because there are some potent planetary positions and aspects in store for you. Now is the time to take a peek at Lady Luck, who isn't at all hard to spot. Any form of limited speculation is right, just as long as your intuition tells you that this is the case.

10 TUESDAY

Moon Age Day 19   Moon Sign Sagittarius

am ....

pm...

There are gains coming along at the moment that you definitely didn't expect. Excellent influences surround love and marriage, so it looks like today is a time when you will be turning to the one you love the most. They, in turn, will show their affection for you, and maybe even in very practical ways.

11 WEDNESDAY

Moon Age Day 20   Moon Sign Sagittarius

am ....

pm...

A burst of excitement at some stage today might be difficult to explain. On the whole, life will seem fairly stable, partly thanks to the position of the Sun as it presently stands in your solar chart. It's true that some things won't be as exciting as they have been but that won't matter as long as you remain content.

12 THURSDAY

Moon Age Day 21   Moon Sign Capricorn

am ....

pm...

Whatever you undertake, you can now do it with aplomb. There are gains to be made at work and maybe a new job in the pipeline if you are between positions. Something very exciting is at hand. Maybe it's a project you started some time ago or it might just be that you are generally anxious to get ahead.

13 FRIDAY
Moon Age Day 22   Moon Sign Capricorn

am ....

pm ....

If you choose to look at money matters today, you should discover that things are coming together even better than you expected. Of course, this depends whether or not you even choose to look at such matters today. Certainly there are plenty of other things that could occupy your mind and you won't be stuck for exciting ways to have a good time.

14 SATURDAY
Moon Age Day 23   Moon Sign Aquarius

am ....

pm ....

In some respects you are more conservative than usual at the moment and might not be at all willing to take the sort of risks that were second-nature a week or two ago. All the same, you should be more than ready now to be making new social contacts and that means you will be welcoming some new friends into your life at any time now.

15 SUNDAY
Moon Age Day 24   Moon Sign Aquarius

am ....

pm ....

Don't be fooled by people telling you what they think is right for you. In all probability you will make it plain to almost everyone that your ideas are the best. There's plenty of scope for having fun today, and you should make time to look ahead optimistically and reassure yourself that things are going to work out the way you want.

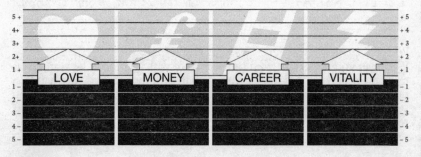

16 MONDAY

Moon Age Day 25   Moon Sign Aquarius

am ....

pm...

If you have decisions to make, you may be tempted to decide pretty much on the toss of a coin. However, even then you will only take calculated risks so that's not such a bad thing. You may be in two minds about a critical decision, most likely to do with work, rather than home or family.

17 TUESDAY

Moon Age Day 26   Moon Sign Pisces

am ....

pm...

Though you are likely to spend rather more than you probably should at this stage of the month, you might also find that some cash is coming in from relatively unexpected directions, which compensates somewhat for what is going out. You can't rely on this trend absolutely, so you should still be careful about too much outlay.

18 WEDNESDAY

Moon Age Day 27   Moon Sign Pisces

am ....

pm...

If you are looking for relaxation today, it's likely to be a very dynamic way of relaxing. Sporting Scorpios are in the best position of all and should be performing well above their personal best. You should be in a much better position now to call the shots, especially if people are relying on you slightly more than usual.

19 THURSDAY

Moon Age Day 28   Moon Sign Aries

am ....

pm...

In all probability, close ties and personal relationships are once again on your mind and prove to be the most important aspects of the day. It is true that as the day advances you will be looking more and more at practical issues and by the evening you could discover reserves of energy you hadn't recognised.

20 FRIDAY

Moon Age Day 29   Moon Sign Aries

am ....

pm ....

You will probably manage to get far more done today than you would have expected and won't be in the least fazed by having to do several different things at the same time. You might have to wait for friends to catch up. Idealism is a powerful component to your nature at the best of times but is especially well marked now.

21 SATURDAY

Moon Age Day 0   Moon Sign Aries

am ....

pm ....

You might find certain tasks you are expected to undertake to be somewhat intimidating but when the time comes, you will handle yourself much better than you might have imagined. You will need to put your domestic and emotional life on the back burner because this is a time to get out there into the social mainstream.

22 SUNDAY

Moon Age Day 1   Moon Sign Taurus

am ....

pm ....

Keep life simple for the next couple of days. If you manage this, then the lunar low will have very little bearing on your life at all. It's time to get intimate and to let your partner know how much they mean to you. Those looking for love could do worse than to keep their eyes wide open around now.

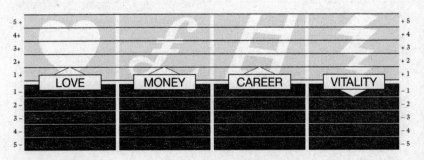

23 MONDAY

Moon Age Day 2   Moon Sign Taurus

am ....

pm ....

Some Scorpians will now be thinking about major changes in terms of home surroundings, with a few even considering the possibility of a change of abode in the near future. This should be a slightly more settled time in financial terms and there is new scope for improvement to the details of your life.

24 TUESDAY

Moon Age Day 3   Moon Sign Gemini

am ....

pm ....

If you need to make any work-based decisions, today could be the best time. You should be on top form in all practical matters although now suddenly less inclined to get involved in deep heart-to-hearts. This change of tack isn't too surprising, bearing in mind planetary trends as they stand.

25 WEDNESDAY

Moon Age Day 4   Moon Sign Gemini

am ....

pm ....

Confrontation with family members is not to be recommended at present, especially since you may be able to get your own way without this. There may well be good things still happening on a practical level, with less consideration being given to the deeper aspects of life that often weigh heavy on the Scorpio mind.

26 THURSDAY

Moon Age Day 5   Moon Sign Gemini

am ....

pm ....

If you play your cards right, you can attract the finer things in life, although you feel a spiritual element to your nature right now that doesn't care very much for possessions. These are conflicting qualities that you have to resolve as best you can. Meanwhile, friends will be urging you to have a splurge of some sort.

27 FRIDAY
Moon Age Day 6   Moon Sign Cancer

am ....

pm ....

Although you might be considering stretching the bounds of possibility, this is probably not a good time for that course of action. There seems to be no better way of getting ahead than by sticking to what you know for the moment. Try keeping to the basics rather than going out on a limb.

28 SATURDAY
Moon Age Day 7   Moon Sign Cancer

am ....

pm ....

The weekend offers a direct contrast to much that has been happening during the week as a whole. Now you are more positive, show a greater general determination and will also be captivated by anything old, unusual or curious. A certain degree of enlightenment comes to many Scorpios at this time.

29 SUNDAY
Moon Age Day 8   Moon Sign Leo

am ....

pm ....

Although you may want to let the whole world know how much you love a certain individual, this might not be the best time to be wearing your heart on your sleeve. Temper your emotions, or at least hide them from people you don't think you can trust. You can look forward to newcomers in your life, especially at a social level.

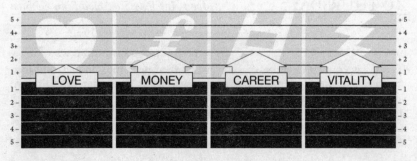

30 MONDAY

Moon Age Day 9   Moon Sign Leo

am ....

pm...

There are potential gains to be made from simply being in the right place at the right time but your deep insights are also part of the scenario. A communication from far away might lift your spirits at the beginning of this week and you will also be chattier than may have been the case for a number of days.

1 TUESDAY

Moon Age Day 10   Moon Sign Virgo

am ....

pm...

The level of physical energy you register today is extremely high. Your spirits are very much alive now and there are many practical gains to be made by simply keeping alert to what is going on around you. If you do that, you should be feeling both happy and confident, plus you'll get plenty of attention from those around you.

2 WEDNESDAY

Moon Age Day 11   Moon Sign Virgo

am ....

pm...

Scorpians who are presently in full-time education can expect to be doing well with their studies now. You can demonstrate today how outgoing and enthusiastic you can be, though you could suffer a little from inadequate planning and will need to be careful if someone you consider a rival is not going to get ahead of you.

3 THURSDAY

Moon Age Day 12   Moon Sign Libra

am ....

pm...

Today is a favourable period for important negotiations and discussions; if you show determination and belief, you should be able to get what you want. You may turn your attention to comfort and security later in the day. The focus for most of the day is on communication issues in the outside world.

4 FRIDAY
Moon Age Day 13   Moon Sign Libra

am..

pm..

You might feel particularly frustrated with some younger people, whose objectives and desires directly contradict your own. Scorpio patience is called for. Domestic matters could tie you down somewhat right now and you would be best not getting too involved in situations you currently can't or won't alter.

5 SATURDAY
Moon Age Day 14   Moon Sign Scorpio

am..

pm..

What matters to you the most now is self determination but be careful that you are not too dismissive of people telling you what you ought to do. The lunar high makes you very positive and inclines you to follow your own ideas, no matter what. Scorpio doesn't do this unless it is very sure of itself and of the prevailing circumstances.

6 SUNDAY
Moon Age Day 15   Moon Sign Scorpio

am..

pm..

High energy levels are the key to today – you should be attacking whatever tasks you have in hand with vigour, which will gain you plenty of attention. That, in turn, should raise your confidence further. Don't take your eye off the ball, though, as it is important that you stay in touch with what is going on around you.

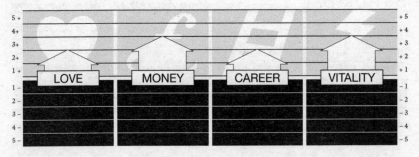

May

2012

YOUR MONTH AT A GLANCE

$\oplus$ = Opportunities are around $\ominus$ = Be on the defensive   ● = Life is pretty ordinary

UNCONSCIOUS IMPULSES

STRENGTH OF PERSONALITY

TEAMWORK ACTIVITIES

PERSONAL FINANCE

$\ominus$

CAREER INSPIRATIONS

$\ominus$

USEFUL INFORMATION GATHERING

$\oplus$ EXTERNAL INFLUENCES/ EDUCATION

$\oplus$ DOMESTIC AFFAIRS

$\oplus$ PLEASURE & ROMANCE

QUESTIONING, THINKING & DECIDING

ONE-TO-ONE RELATIONSHIPS

EFFECTIVE WORK & HEALTH

MAY HIGHS AND LOWS

Here I show you how the rhythms of the Moon will affect you this month. Like the tide, your energies and abilities will rise and fall with its pattern. When it is above the centre line, go for it, when it is below, you should be resting.

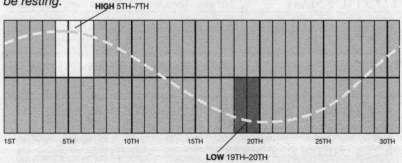

HIGH 5TH–7TH

1ST   5TH   10TH   15TH   20TH   25TH   30TH

LOW 19TH–20TH

7 MONDAY
Moon Age Day 16   Moon Sign Scorpio

am ....

pm...

It is definitely worth talking, talking and talking again in order to get what you want. Although not everyone is on your side, you should be confident in your ability to persuade others to follow your lead. You can afford to be slightly more ambitious than usual in your personal aims and should be going for gold at every possible opportunity.

8 TUESDAY
Moon Age Day 17   Moon Sign Sagittarius

am ....

pm...

Sooner or later there are issues that you are going to have to face and it might as well be now as at any time later. Some of the responsibilities coming to you from the outside world won't be very welcome and you could decide to retreat into yourself a little at the moment.

9 WEDNESDAY
Moon Age Day 18   Moon Sign Sagittarius

am ....

pm...

Woe betide anyone who tries to force you into any sort of mould right now because it just won't work. Have some patience with family members who are going slightly astray and listen to them. You will certainly have to summon up some patience with financial restrictions because your main aim will be more, not less, freedom.

10 THURSDAY
Moon Age Day 19   Moon Sign Capricorn

am ....

pm...

Trends suggest that you may now be researching something or perhaps be involved in higher education. If so, make certain that you concentrate your efforts because that could lead to a significant breakthrough. Communication matters put you in the picture today so it is very important to keep talking – to anyone who will listen and respond.

11 FRIDAY
Moon Age Day 20   Moon Sign Capricorn

am ....

pm ....

There are people around at work who are very influenced by what you have to say and you can use that to move matters forward quite progressively. Even casual conversations can have far-reaching implications. This would be an excellent time in which to put your powers of persuasion to work.

12 SATURDAY
Moon Age Day 21   Moon Sign Aquarius

am ....

pm ....

Concern for family members, which could have been running quite high of late, is not so marked at present, leaving you extra time to spend doing what suits you personally. Personal and domestic concerns now bring out the best in you, though there are social bonuses around too, probably later in the day.

13 SUNDAY
Moon Age Day 22   Moon Sign Aquarius

am ....

pm ....

Your focus should be on routines and you will be happiest surrounded by familiar people and things – strangers are not likely to figure in your life. The need for excitement and change hasn't gone away, it's simply been put on hold for a while. The most important involvements today are with people you know well.

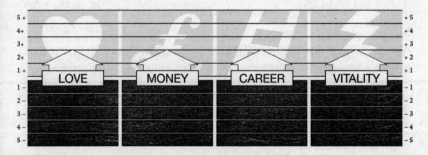

14 MONDAY
Moon Age Day 23   Moon Sign Pisces

am ....

pm ....

Suddenly the emphasis is on busy communication, though others might find you just a little too talkative at the moment. It's important not to labour points too much and if you remember the general rule for now – which is to spread yourself around as much as you can – you won't go far wrong. A friend may need some very specific advice.

15 TUESDAY
Moon Age Day 24   Moon Sign Pisces

am ....

pm ....

Today would be fine for all those little domestic chores that have been piling up and you should also find moments to spend with your partner or family members. You can benefit from finding yourself in the middle of a day that is far less demanding than some of the ones you have experienced of late.

16 WEDNESDAY
Moon Age Day 25   Moon Sign Aries

am ....

pm ....

There is no doubt that you are presently well equipped to make friends and influence people, even if the incentive to do so isn't quite as strong today as it has been recently. In addition to your personable streak, there is also a very private Scorpio showing. The combination might be difficult for some people to understand.

17 THURSDAY
Moon Age Day 26   Moon Sign Aries

am ....

pm ....

Keeping up with the Joneses isn't something that is as important to you as it is to those with you live with. You are out to show the world that you know what you are talking about but it's very important that you are sure this is genuinely the case. Check all your details and make this a time to undertake some essential research.

18 FRIDAY
Moon Age Day 27   Moon Sign Aries

am ....

pm..

Turn on your charm today and you could turn a few heads. You seem to have the secret of popularity at the moment because, even without trying, you can make a good impression. Actually you are quite a magnetic person and you are probably the only individual around who doesn't realise this fact.

19 SATURDAY
Moon Age Day 28   Moon Sign Taurus

am ....

pm..

Your daily life could become somewhat disorganised, to say the least. The culprit is the lunar low, though it also brings a good deal of amusement this time round as you discover just how funny you can be when things start to go haywire. There is little or no animosity in your life right now, which is comfortable and gratifying.

20 SUNDAY
Moon Age Day 0   Moon Sign Taurus

am ....

pm..

This is a time to think and to clear the decks for new actions in the days ahead. You may actively choose to spend time in solitary contemplation, and this would be sensible as your power to control the direction of your life is temporarily diminished. Be reassured, though, that this situation is only temporary.

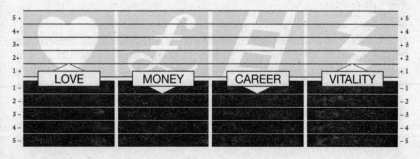

21 MONDAY
Moon Age Day 1   Moon Sign Gemini

am...

pm...

You should be feeling really confident and that will give you the secret of success that very few people have. If you don't trust your own luck, then you might not make the most of it, so it is important to believe in yourself. Today you know you are number one.

22 TUESDAY
Moon Age Day 2   Moon Sign Gemini

am...

pm...

You have the ability to turn drudgery into pleasure today. Don't be put off by obstacles around this time because you will soon overcome them. It's true that some situations look potentially troublesome but once you roll up your sleeves and pitch in, nothing could be further from the truth.

23 WEDNESDAY
Moon Age Day 3   Moon Sign Gemini

am...

pm...

You may be expected to take a lead in some new projects and, though you might find yourself just a little nervous, in the end you are almost certain to come good. The need for your personal input is clearly paramount at present so don't hold back when it comes to putting forward your point of view.

24 THURSDAY
Moon Age Day 4   Moon Sign Cancer

am...

pm...

If it seems that nothing particularly exciting is happening at present, the reason could be that you aren't adding enough input. You can use this period in order to rise to the challenges you face and there isn't anything preventing you from putting in that extra bit of effort that really counts.

25 FRIDAY
Moon Age Day 5   Moon Sign Cancer

am ....

pm..

There are likely to be some gifts coming your way, even though some of these will turn out to be very different from what you may have expected. Keep a cool head when it matters the most. Decision-making is easy and this is the time of the month during which you can make up your mind quickly and decisively.

26 SATURDAY
Moon Age Day 6   Moon Sign Leo

am ....

pm..

What an amazing time this would be to take a trip and particularly a holiday. If you can't do that, then just have a good time where you are. On the other hand, you also recognise that there is a serious side to life and you are pushing just as hard as you can to get ahead at the start of the weekend.

27 SUNDAY
Moon Age Day 7   Moon Sign Leo

am ....

pm..

You won't be short of excellent ideas, though putting them into practice won't be quite as easy as you might have wished. However, you should feel enough confidence to persevere when it really counts at work. Communication once again proves to be your main area of satisfaction, as has been the case throughout much of May.

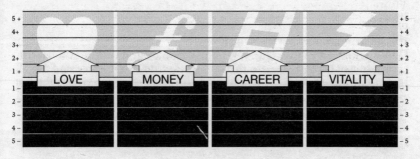

28 MONDAY

Moon Age Day 8   Moon Sign Leo

am ....

pm...

In some respects you could find yourself entering a slightly lazy streak around now. All the same, a drive to renew things is at hand. Maybe you are thinking about trading in your car, or considering a new sofa for your house. Whatever it might be, shop around in order to make sure you get the best bargain possible.

29 TUESDAY

Moon Age Day 9   Moon Sign Virgo

am ....

pm...

It could be that today is a real patience tester and you can blame present planetary trends for this. Don't allow yourself to become annoyed at people who seem determined to be dense. As long as you retain your sense of humour and your ability to see things with your unique perspective, awkward trends won't last.

30 WEDNESDAY

Moon Age Day 10   Moon Sign Virgo

am ....

pm...

The attitude of your partner might be somewhat difficult to understand but not once you have asked the right questions. Stay away from pointless rules and silly regulations. The desire to please others is extremely strong and this is especially true where friends are concerned.

31 THURSDAY

Moon Age Day 11   Moon Sign Libra

am ....

pm...

Don't get involved in family rows if you can avoid it, but if you have no choice, make certain you are the one who settles them once and for all. If you work hard today, you can gain time to spend on yourself at the weekend. Organise a social outing or two and make sure you plan well ahead when it comes to general breaks or holidays.

1 FRIDAY
Moon Age Day 12   Moon Sign Libra

am ....

pm ....

Relations with family members are now strengthened by a number of astrological factors and if there is something you need to ask for in the way of a favour, this could be the best time of all in which to do it. Relying on friends can be less advisable for today at least because they may be too busy to lend assistance.

2 SATURDAY
Moon Age Day 13   Moon Sign Scorpio

am ....

pm ....

You need to follow your instincts today because with a host of supporting planetary positions, together with the lunar high, you shouldn't go wrong. This can be a really interesting sort of day and one packed with variety. Fresh starts are a must, together with new ways of looking at old situations.

3 SUNDAY
Moon Age Day 14   Moon Sign Scorpio

am ....

pm ....

The attitude of colleagues especially is likely to be surprising and more than useful. Friends are demanding but sweet. Don't be afraid to aim high or to take some chances once the week gets started. You could find yourself on a very important springboard and with a very positive sort of week in front of you – it's time to jump.

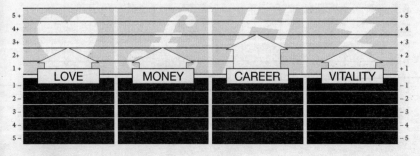

June

2012

YOUR MONTH AT A GLANCE

⊕ = Opportunities are around   ⊖ = Be on the defensive   ⬤ = Life is pretty ordinary

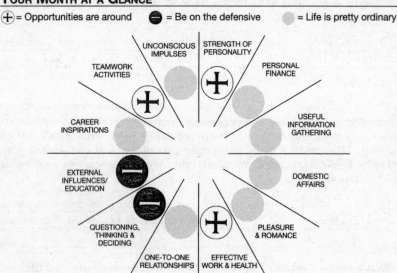

UNCONSCIOUS IMPULSES

STRENGTH OF PERSONALITY

TEAMWORK ACTIVITIES

PERSONAL FINANCE

CAREER INSPIRATIONS

USEFUL INFORMATION GATHERING

EXTERNAL INFLUENCES/ EDUCATION

DOMESTIC AFFAIRS

QUESTIONING, THINKING & DECIDING

PLEASURE & ROMANCE

ONE-TO-ONE RELATIONSHIPS

EFFECTIVE WORK & HEALTH

JUNE HIGHS AND LOWS

Here I show you how the rhythms of the Moon will affect you this month. Like the tide, your energies and abilities will rise and fall with its pattern. When it is above the centre line, go for it, when it is below, you should be resting.

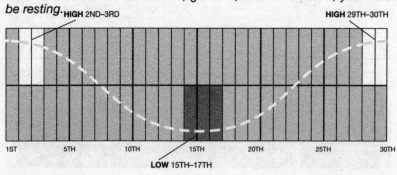

HIGH 2ND–3RD

HIGH 29TH–30TH

1ST   5TH   10TH   15TH   20TH   25TH   30TH

LOW 15TH–17TH

4 MONDAY
Moon Age Day 15   Moon Sign Sagittarius

am ....

pm...

You may not get exactly what you want in a professional sense today but you can be sure that those you care about the most are showing a great deal of affection and can give you plenty of support. The domestic scene tends to be not only fairly hectic but also quite rewarding.

5 TUESDAY
Moon Age Day 16   Moon Sign Sagittarius

am ....

pm...:...

Try to put yourself in the company of people you find stimulating and exciting later in the day, and it will give you a huge boost and make you feel, and even look, more attractive. In the meantime you might have to put up with second best but since your desires are few, that won't be a problem either.

6 WEDNESDAY
Moon Age Day 17   Moon Sign Capricorn

am ....

pm...

Don't rise to the bait of someone who is spoiling for a row and then you will be the winner from the word go. At work you may need to do the same job more than once. A period of intense feelings and emotional conflicts is now at hand, though this will have less impact on your life if you are aware of its presence.

7 THURSDAY
Moon Age Day 18   Moon Sign Capricorn

am ....

pm...

Routines could seem quite comfortable at a time when you probably won't want to be pushing your horizons too much. You need to get on top of work matters as soon as you can this morning. If this isn't possible, you might have to rely on the help of someone else to apply order and organisation.

8 FRIDAY
Moon Age Day 19   Moon Sign Aquarius

am...

pm...

If they stopped to think about the situation, some people might accuse you of being undisciplined at present. They probably think you are not concentrating on those matters that seem to be the most important. However, they don't live your life and you should only take notice if you know they are right.

9 SATURDAY
Moon Age Day 20   Moon Sign Aquarius

am...

pm...

People you don't see every day are now likely to be cropping up in your life all the time and you might also be invited to take part in something that has been a mystery to you in the past. Be careful that you are not taken in by others; show a little caution and don't be quite as trusting as might sometimes be the case.

10 SUNDAY
Moon Age Day 21   Moon Sign Pisces

am...

pm...

This is not a day during which practical or professional matters should be allowed to get in the way of simply doing what seems like special fun. You need to find time today to go off and explore the world as much as you can. There is plenty to see and any number of interesting people around.

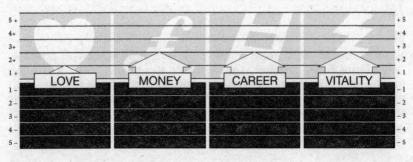

11 MONDAY
Moon Age Day 22   Moon Sign Pisces

am ....

pm...

Your persuasive powers are very good at the moment and you can be of special use to a family member who has been having problems of late because the way you look at life and your sense of fun are very infectious. You may have exciting and unusual social and romantic possibilities before you so stay alert.

12 TUESDAY
Moon Age Day 23   Moon Sign Pisces

am ....

pm...

Even though you feel you are doing very well, it is possible that someone will not believe you are pulling your weight and you should put in some extra effort to convince them. In fact, you have nothing to prove. This would be a very good time for co-operative and collaborative endeavours of almost any sort.

13 WEDNESDAY
Moon Age Day 24   Moon Sign Aries

am ....

pm...

Planetary influences suggest that you should not take anything too seriously, and actively take a break from responsibility if you get the chance. Don't focus on your limitations or they will come to the fore. Simply be yourself and go with the flow. Social events ought to be both easy-going and enjoyable over the next few days.

14 THURSDAY
Moon Age Day 25   Moon Sign Aries

am ....

pm...

Certain compromises can be rather more difficult than you would wish. In the end you could decide that you are better off sticking to your guns, especially in professional matters. It may be that people don't give you time to think things through clearly, which means there isn't quite as much manoeuvring room as you need.

15 FRIDAY
Moon Age Day 26   Moon Sign Taurus

am ....

pm..

You now have to endure the three days of the lunar low that come along at this time. In fact, this month this need not be a trial at all. Just remember to stay away from anything sensational and don't take unnecessary risks. You might find quiet pursuits more interesting in any case whilst present trends are in place.

16 SATURDAY
Moon Age Day 27   Moon Sign Taurus

am ....

pm..

This could be another day during which you won't feel like competing as much as has been the case during the last few weeks. Have a rest and take the opportunity to look around. Confidence is low but you are already planning some sort of coup for later and as long as you don't try to push ahead now, all should be well.

17 SUNDAY
Moon Age Day 28   Moon Sign Taurus

am ....

pm..

You may retire into yourself at some stage today but you are merely reacting to the temporary position of the Moon. Don't be too quick to take offence, especially with a friend. Though your personal life can be somewhat unsettled, by tomorrow everything is going to look very different, so it is important not to overreact.

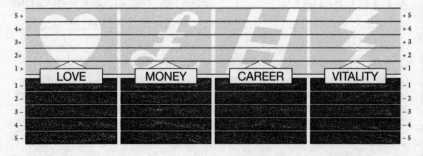

18 MONDAY   *Moon Age Day 29   Moon Sign Gemini*

am ....

pm...

A new understanding is possible with someone you haven't always understood well. You may have occasion to share your feelings and emotions quite freely and openly at the moment and feel you have nothing to hide. Your attitude can be quite disarming as far as those around you are concerned and you will probably discover that they respond by being equally truthful.

19 TUESDAY   *Moon Age Day 0   Moon Sign Gemini*

am ....

pm...

There are possible romantic overtures for some today, as well as some social surprises. This may not be the most dynamic or materially successful stage of the month but it can be quite gratifying and happy. Bring your focus on to the family and make it your priority because much of this part of the week is likely to be spent in their company.

20 WEDNESDAY   *Moon Age Day 1   Moon Sign Cancer*

am ....

pm...

This is likely to be a day of busy demands and responsibilities so it would be good to find a little time to yourself at some stage during the day. Fortunately you are in the right state of mind to take such a day in your stride, working through a mountain of tasks slowly and steadily.

21 THURSDAY   *Moon Age Day 2   Moon Sign Cancer*

am ....

pm...

Not only do you shine when in company today but you should also discover talents you didn't know you possessed. There's more coming along than you bargained for, most likely in a very positive way. Don't leave anything to chance today and make sure that everyone knows you are around. This is an important day in more than one respect.

22 FRIDAY
Moon Age Day 3   Moon Sign Cancer

am...

pm...

The attitude of your family and friends presently makes it that much easier to gain their trust and co-operation in anything. You have the potential to make great gains at work, particularly since you are presently willing to take the sort of chances you might have shied away from only a short time ago.

23 SATURDAY
Moon Age Day 4   Moon Sign Leo

am...

pm...

Almost like a bolt from the blue, you may experience a strong sense of nostalgia around at this time, leading you to spend as much time today looking back as you do forward. This contrasts markedly with your desire to get ahead and so some conflict tends to crop up within your mind today. Resolve these issues by talking about them.

24 SUNDAY
Moon Age Day 5   Moon Sign Leo

am...

pm...

You are now well over two-thirds of the way through the month and you still haven't done some of the things that seemed important two or three weeks ago. Now is the time to assess the way situations are unfolding and to offer the extra assistance that is going to be necessary to get new plans off the ground.

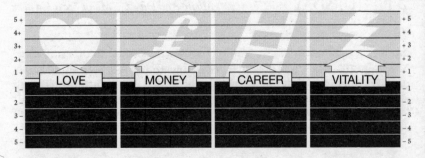

25 MONDAY
Moon Age Day 6   Moon Sign Virgo

am ....

pm..

Although today is likely to be extremely busy, you should make the time to let those around you know how important they are to you and just what their assistance in your life really means. This is a period during which you can focus your mind more clearly than has been the case for several months and you can take some decisive action.

26 TUESDAY
Moon Age Day 7   Moon Sign Virgo

am ....

pm..

Not everyone seems to be on your side at present, though the most important people will be. You feel energetic and strong, which is why you could be so adventurous. You may even be surprised at your own tenacity and bravery, leading you to little adventures you can really enjoy.

27 WEDNESDAY
Moon Age Day 8   Moon Sign Libra

am ....

pm..

Keep an eye open for opportunities that mean new investments, though do bear in mind that you need to think in terms of the more distant future. There are some promising financial developments about and you should try to make the most of them when you can. Romance is well starred today.

28 THURSDAY
Moon Age Day 9   Moon Sign Libra

am ....

pm..

The best incentives are still a day or so away and you could waste a lot of energy today but get nowhere. Instead, spend time with your lover or with family members and friends and forget achievement for now. Although today looks as though it could turn out to be rather busy, in reality you would be better off getting some rest.

29 FRIDAY
Moon Age Day 10   Moon Sign Scorpio

am ....

pm ....

It might be said that luck is on your side today but the simple fact is that you are making your own luck as you go along. Don't be shy when it comes to showing others what you are capable of achieving and do be willing to share your new views regarding work with colleagues and bosses alike. Enjoy the lunar high.

30 SATURDAY
Moon Age Day 11   Moon Sign Scorpio

am ....

pm ....

There hasn't been a better day as far as you are concerned for some weeks past. You feel as though you could run the world single-handedly. A slight exaggeration, perhaps, but nonetheless you are capable of making good decisions. After work, do your best to have some unrestricted fun.

1 SUNDAY
Moon Age Day 12   Moon Sign Sagittarius

am ....

pm ....

Try explaining the way you feel about things in order to bring you to a better understanding of yourself. A lively sociability seems to prevail as you get yourself ready to embark on another working week. There probably won't be anything extraordinary about today but it does have its positive moments, not least in love so make the most of these.

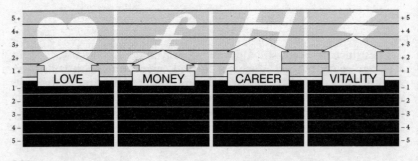

July

2012

Your Month at a Glance

⊕ = Opportunities are around   ⊖ = Be on the defensive   ● = Life is pretty ordinary

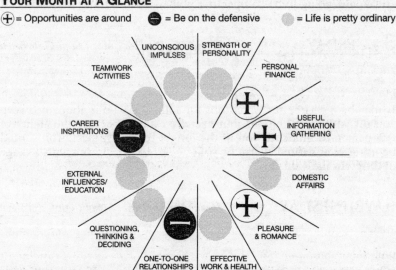

July Highs and Lows

Here I show you how the rhythms of the Moon will affect you this month. Like the tide, your energies and abilities will rise and fall with its pattern. When it is above the centre line, go for it, when it is below, you should be resting.

HIGH 27TH–28TH

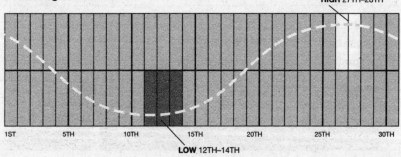

1ST   5TH   10TH   15TH   20TH   25TH   30TH

LOW 12TH–14TH

2 MONDAY
Moon Age Day 13   Moon Sign Sagittarius

am ....

pm...

Daily life should have plenty to keep you both occupied and interested at the beginning of a new and active week. Rules and regulations are easy to deal with – you should simply ignore them if they get in your way. Not everyone is going to be co-operative now so stick to those who are.

3 TUESDAY
Moon Age Day 14   Moon Sign Capricorn

am ....

pm...

It may be a cliché, but watch out for someone who is about to sweep you off your feet. Enjoy it, but exercise caution because the ability of this person to influence you in the longer term is suspect. You should be using your natural charm or your ability to get on well with a range of different individuals.

4 WEDNESDAY
Moon Age Day 15   Moon Sign Capricorn

am ....

pm...

When you are not dealing with the mundane, you could find your mind wandering to some interesting and far-away places. Try to bring your focus back to practical details, especially at work. You should enlist the support of people you haven't been close to before and might even make one or two new friends.

5 THURSDAY
Moon Age Day 16   Moon Sign Capricorn

am ....

pm...

In sporting and social activities alike, this is clearly a time to go for gold as you are feeling positive and powerful, but you do need to avoid being sidetracked by matters that are of no real importance. There is a danger that you could be too indecisive with regard to some issues you are facing.

6 FRIDAY
Moon Age Day 17   Moon Sign Aquarius

am ....

pm..

Things are looking good. You are at the peak of your powers today, both mentally and probably physically. This might lead you on a fitness regime or down the road to other improvements you think are necessary. It would be sensible to plan such matters carefully rather than being too impulsive.

7 SATURDAY
Moon Age Day 18   Moon Sign Aquarius

am ....

pm..

There is great potential for visiting new places around this time so it would be a good time to go on a trip. Meanwhile you could be demonstrating great sympathy for the underdog, but that's just the sort of person you are. However, you should take care not to give those around you the impression that you are some sort of sucker.

8 SUNDAY
Moon Age Day 19   Moon Sign Pisces

am ....

pm..

Variety is important today. The harder you work to improve your general financial situation at this time, the greater are the rewards that come in later. However, you also need excitement in your life around now and would be quite unwilling to sit around the house all day, counting your money and checking your bank statements.

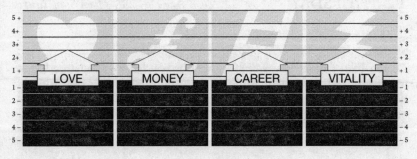

MONDAY *Moon Age Day 20   Moon Sign Pisces*

am..

pm..

Today you should discover that affairs of the heart are going the way you would wish, and you should look out for opportunities for a new relationship. Success in money matters might take more hard work than you expect but you are quite shrewd and inclined to do whatever is necessary to get on financially.

10 TUESDAY *Moon Age Day 21   Moon Sign Aries*

am..

pm..

Be careful of mechanical gadgets, one or two of which could be causing you minor problems around this time. The personal attitude of friends can be puzzling later in the day. Affairs of the heart are well accented and the sign of Scorpio is showing an even more than usually spirited response to many aspects of life.

11 WEDNESDAY *Moon Age Day 22   Moon Sign Aries*

am..

pm..

All of a sudden there is little room for speculation, you should hang on to your money for the moment and also shelve a few social commitments for a few days. You may have to forego certain pleasures around now in order to concentrate on matters that seem particularly important on a personal level.

12 THURSDAY *Moon Age Day 23   Moon Sign Taurus*

am..

pm..

Thanks to the lunar low, a few of the jobs you feel you must undertake today turn out to be hard work. There is no other real reason why this should be the case and it might be best simply to have a rest for today. If that proves possible, stick to things you like and undertake tasks one at a time for the best results.

13 FRIDAY
Moon Age Day 24   Moon Sign Taurus

am ....

pm ....

Be careful about investing large sums of money around now and if it is necessary for you to sign any sort of document, do so after careful thought. You will have to get one or two tedious jobs out of the way early in the day if you want to gain in the longer-term with social possibilities. Even then, tomorrow will be better.

14 SATURDAY
Moon Age Day 25   Moon Sign Taurus

am ....

pm ....

Try to use the power of positive thought to create the sort of future you want the most. Although putting such thoughts into action might have to wait for a couple of days, there is nothing to prevent you from planning carefully and from reaching a stage in your thinking that gets you over a psychological hurdle.

15 SUNDAY
☿   *Moon Age Day 26   Moon Sign Gemini*

am ....

pm ....

Trends suggest that anything curious, old or even odd is grist to your mill today. Communication matters see you on top form and prove that you have no difficulty at all getting your message across to almost anyone with whom you communicate. There may also be advantages to be gained through looking at life in a novel way.

16 MONDAY ☿ *Moon Age Day 27 Moon Sign Gemini*

am ....

pm ....

Do the things you really want to do today and not what you are expected to do. You may find you have a change of heart over a personal matter. Material and financial issues should be looking more settled, leading you to the feeling that you can spend more time thinking about romance and relationships.

17 TUESDAY ☿ *Moon Age Day 28 Moon Sign Gemini*

am ....

pm ....

If not everyone takes the notice of you that you would wish, just focus your efforts on those who do. Routines are not especially stimulating now and you need to look for variety. Leisure and pleasure are emphasised for much of the time, and you will be happiest if you can remain the centre of attention.

18 WEDNESDAY ☿ *Moon Age Day 29 Moon Sign Cancer*

am ....

pm ....

Scorpio can be a strange sign because there are times when you would run a mile rather than be in the public gaze but other times, like now, when you positively preen yourself in full view. This is a high-spirited period and a time during which you will be making every move to stay in the spotlight.

19 THURSDAY ☿ *Moon Age Day 0 Moon Sign Cancer*

am ....

pm ....

Our state of mind has a huge impact on our lives. If you believe you are equal to a particular task, you most probably are. Today you should be pushing the boundaries of your expectation of yourself because you are so enthusiastic and competitive. Even you might be surprised at how well you perform.

20 FRIDAY ☿ *Moon Age Day 1   Moon Sign Leo*

am ....

pm...

You'll feel so energetic and industrious that you should be choosing to work hard today – in fact, it may not seem like work at all. Look again at objectives that might have seemed impossible only months ago and apply your determination and vigour to make them happen.

21 SATURDAY ☿ *Moon Age Day 2   Moon Sign Leo*

am ....

pm...

There won't be much difficulty in coming to terms with practical issues but from an emotional point of view you may be rather too sensitive for your own good. If you can, settle for some way of enjoying yourself that is not too physically demanding. Focus on relationships today, and especially those that are most important to you.

22 SUNDAY ☿ *Moon Age Day 3   Moon Sign Virgo*

am ....

pm...

If you have nothing but leisure in front of you, there is a strong possibility that you will turn even this into a sort of work, maybe in the garden or decorating your home. Career issues could have their own pitfalls at the moment, which is why Scorpio subjects who do not work at a weekend are the luckiest now.

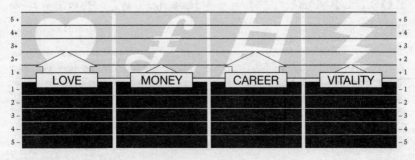

23 MONDAY ☿ *Moon Age Day 4   Moon Sign Virgo*

am...

pm...

Scorpians always consider how their actions affect those around them so there's only a slim chance that some Scorpios might upset someone today. If that happens, do try to explain yourself fully. Working in conjunction with others, you can now come up with some really good plans and will also have the chance to put them into action.

24 TUESDAY ☿ *Moon Age Day 5   Moon Sign Libra*

am...

pm...

Meet as many different people as you can at the moment and make the most of extremely good trends that involve doing little more than enjoying yourself with others. A new social contact or an existing friend might do you a great favour now and you will need to think up a unique way of saying thank you.

25 WEDNESDAY ☿ *Moon Age Day 6   Moon Sign Libra*

am...

pm...

Explaining yourself and your ideas as fully as you can is now extremely important. Someone you don't see very often is likely to be making an appearance and there might be the opportunity to make a trip that is planned at very short notice. Above all, don't let others get hold of the wrong end of the stick at this time.

26 THURSDAY ☿ *Moon Age Day 7   Moon Sign Libra*

am...

pm...

You should find you are filled with excellent ideas so make sure you put them into practice, then you won't feel obliged to conform to other people's expectations, which won't please you. There should be plenty of good company around socially, and you should look out for some good opportunities for gain, both in a material and a personal sense.

27 FRIDAY ☿ *Moon Age Day 8 Moon Sign Scorpio*

am ....

pm ....

Generally speaking, you should find your level of luck extremely high at the moment. Although this won't incline you to go out and put your shirt on the horse running in the next race, you can afford to speculate a good deal more than would usually be the case. Look out for some interesting compliments coming your way.

28 SATURDAY ☿ *Moon Age Day 9 Moon Sign Scorpio*

am ....

pm ....

Thanks to the lunar high, you could do well to re-examine some old problems as you could well come up with new solutions. Being particularly innovative and inspiring in the way you think will influence others, too. All in all, this can turn out to be one of the most stimulating and interesting of days.

29 SUNDAY ☿ *Moon Age Day 10 Moon Sign Sagittarius*

am ....

pm ....

Acting on impulse is now quite important, though you might want to check one or two facts along the way. Romance is on the cards for some Scorpians and your general popularity is assured. Someone is likely to oppose you at this time, and you will almost certainly find that frustrating and annoying – deal with it!

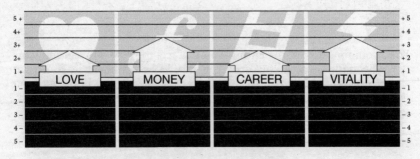

30 MONDAY ☿ *Moon Age Day 11   Moon Sign Sagittarius*

am ....

pm..

You could possibly be spending more time at work than with your partner or loved ones, but at least your time at work should be productive. Specific trends can now make you somewhat absent-minded so it's important to make a note of birthdays or anniversaries that might be in the offing between now and next weekend.

31 TUESDAY ☿ *Moon Age Day 12   Moon Sign Capricorn*

am ....

pm..

Family members should prove not only supportive but will actively encourage your sometimes strange ideas. This might prove to be a day on which you would rather do anything than cause a fuss. That could be a shame because if people are behaving in an unreasonable manner, they need to be told.

1 WEDNESDAY ☿ *Moon Age Day 13   Moon Sign Capricorn*

am ....

pm..

Don't be too quick to jump to conclusions, especially in relationships. If you do, and allow your jealousy to show, you might end up regretting the fact and having to apologise. A fast pace of events in the social world could leave you quite dizzy but still enjoying what life has to offer.

2 THURSDAY ☿ *Moon Age Day 14   Moon Sign Aquarius*

am ....

pm..

You should put to use the enthusiasm you feel for new projects and your overwhelming desire to succeed. You should be confident in your own ability, especially when you know what is expected of you. Look out for a period of increased social activity and the possibility of romantic overtures.

3 FRIDAY ☿ *Moon Age Day 15   Moon Sign Aquarius*

am...

pm...

This should be a very good day for job-related endeavours but also for showing what sporting acumen you have. Don't be too quick to criticise a friend or colleague. Someone older than you or in a position of authority may prove to be a strong motivating force in your life at present.

4 SATURDAY ☿ *Moon Age Day 16   Moon Sign Pisces*

am...

pm...

They say that every journey starts with the first step and this is exactly what you are doing now, moving slowly but steadily towards your objectives. The next couple of days should be fun but prepare for some surprises as they could also be unpredictable. Make the most of this period by being expansive about future ideas and dreams.

5 SUNDAY ☿ *Moon Age Day 17   Moon Sign Pisces*

am...

pm...

The message for today is don't hide your light under a bushel. Although some of your apparent confidence is little more than a pretence, nobody will realise the fact. When it comes to dealing with practical tasks you are second to none today, which is why everyone else will be turning to you for assistance.

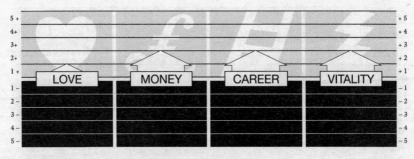

August

2012

YOUR MONTH AT A GLANCE

⊕ = Opportunities are around　⊖ = Be on the defensive　● = Life is pretty ordinary

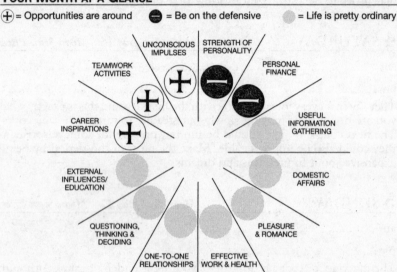

UNCONSCIOUS IMPULSES

STRENGTH OF PERSONALITY

TEAMWORK ACTIVITIES

PERSONAL FINANCE

CAREER INSPIRATIONS

USEFUL INFORMATION GATHERING

EXTERNAL INFLUENCES/ EDUCATION

DOMESTIC AFFAIRS

QUESTIONING, THINKING & DECIDING

PLEASURE & ROMANCE

ONE-TO-ONE RELATIONSHIPS

EFFECTIVE WORK & HEALTH

AUGUST HIGHS AND LOWS

Here I show you how the rhythms of the Moon will affect you this month. Like the tide, your energies and abilities will rise and fall with its pattern. When it is above the centre line, go for it, when it is below, you should be resting.

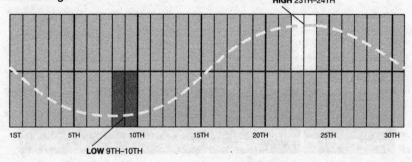

HIGH 23TH–24TH

1ST　5TH　10TH　15TH　20TH　25TH　30TH

LOW 9TH–10TH

6 MONDAY ☿ *Moon Age Day 18   Moon Sign Aries*

am...

pm...

There are gains to be made as a result of looking ahead in the way that Scorpio does well. You could also benefit simply from listening to what is being said around you. You should now be doing as much as you can to enlarge your list of contacts. The more friends you have at the moment, the better.

7 TUESDAY ☿ *Moon Age Day 19   Moon Sign Aries*

am...

pm...

As far as contacts generally are concerned, and agreements you make with them, this period can do you a great deal of good. Some may have difficulty in keeping up with your razor-sharp wit at present and you might have to explain yourself. Look out for a period of great mental inspiration and excitement.

8 WEDNESDAY ☿ *Moon Age Day 20   Moon Sign Aries*

am...

pm...

Mistakes made now could take a while to put right, leaving you feeling that you should have done better in the first place, so tread cautiously. On the other hand, you would do well to take up opportunities to travel. You may be enthusiastically pursuing your ambitions but don't rush your fences.

9 THURSDAY *Moon Age Day 21   Moon Sign Taurus*

am...

pm...

Some Scorpians will negate this particular lunar low altogether by simply turning their attention in different directions. With just a little thought you could be one of them. Your general spirits and your capacity for success might be slightly diminished but this is a very temporary thing and you need to realise this fact.

10 FRIDAY
Moon Age Day 22   Moon Sign Taurus

am..

pm..

You might have to go over a recent project again quite carefully and this is a time when things need looking at with a good deal of scrutiny. It isn't that you are making mistakes, more that you insist on having everything just right. This could be something of a tall order with the lunar low still around.

11 SATURDAY
Moon Age Day 23   Moon Sign Gemini

am..

pm..

Your interests tend to turn towards cultural matters at this particular time. You have a very sensitive quality that you can display to make others sit up and take notice. As is often the case for you, anything old, unusual or downright odd is likely to attract your attention as you turn up your intuition beam too high.

12 SUNDAY
Moon Age Day 24   Moon Sign Gemini

am..

pm..

Your self-confidence is on the increase again and you can use this to your advantage whether or not you are at work. Try looking ahead with renewed determination and you can leave behind the lunar low once and for all. It's commitment all the way from now.

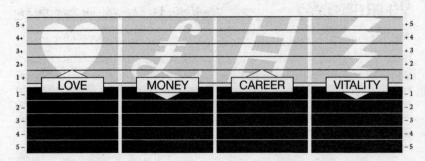

13 MONDAY
Moon Age Day 25   Moon Sign Gemini

am ....

pm ....

This is a time during which you should be able to get a great deal from your career and you should be fairly satisfied with your efforts. Get yourself in amongst groups who have the ability to make you feel special. Pull out all the stops and get busy on current projects in your professional life.

14 TUESDAY
Moon Age Day 26   Moon Sign Cancer

am ....

pm ....

It might occur to you today to do something that you haven't managed to achieve in the past and the effort should prove to be extremely rewarding. Co-operation is more than agreeable today, during a phase that finds you at one with your environment and probably more contented than would normally be the case.

15 WEDNESDAY
Moon Age Day 27   Moon Sign Cancer

am ....

pm ....

In a romantic sense, it is likely that you are on the receiving end of compliments you simply didn't expect. The need to assert yourself and to debate issues is quite strong at the start of this week. Don't allow this to turn into an argumentative phase because this won't do you any good at all.

16 THURSDAY
Moon Age Day 28   Moon Sign Leo

am ....

pm ....

Be bold and determined today and listen to the very sensible advice of people who are older or more experienced than you are. Right now you should be planning ahead in order to make something important possible. Although it might take you some time to work out what this might be, the effort is certainly worthwhile.

17 FRIDAY
Moon Age Day 0   Moon Sign Leo

am ....

pm...

Don't get upset about things not turning out exactly as you might have wished in a social sense. Impromptu plans might prove to be even better. Friendships should be particularly rewarding today and you have everything you need in order to enjoy yourself.

18 SATURDAY
Moon Age Day 1   Moon Sign Leo

am ....

pm...

Don't be in the least surprised if you discover your popularity suddenly soaring. For much of the time today you will want to get down to brass tacks and will be quite keen to get to the bottom of situations that have puzzled you for a while. Ask the right questions and make sure you stay where the action is.

19 SUNDAY
Moon Age Day 2   Moon Sign Virgo

am ....

pm...

What you have on your side today is great cheerfulness and a fairly high opinion of your own capabilities. Good news is likely to arrive around now and it might come from a long way off. However, you need to remain cautious and this is no time for Scorpio to count its chickens before they have hatched.

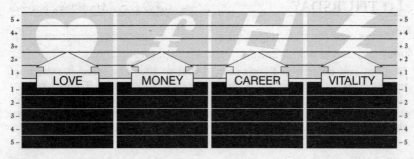

20 MONDAY
Moon Age Day 3   Moon Sign Virgo

am..

pm..

This would be an excellent time to travel and if you have planned your holidays around now, then so much the better. Rules and regulations are likely to get on your nerves, unless you are making them. There should be much about family life that will keep you reassured and happy with your lot.

21 TUESDAY
Moon Age Day 4   Moon Sign Libra

am..

pm..

Your love life is positively highlighted right now and you will find that it is easy to get on the right side of the people who matter. The power of your personality is now boosted by present planetary positions. If there is something you really want, especially in a practical sense, this is the time to be asking for it.

22 WEDNESDAY
Moon Age Day 5   Moon Sign Libra

am..

pm..

Today should bring opportunities to spend some time in the sun and you should try to organise a change of scene and time away from the practical aspects of life. There might be a bit of a lull generally, allowing you more time to please yourself and finding you slightly less committed than has been the case so far this month.

23 THURSDAY
Moon Age Day 6   Moon Sign Scorpio

am..

pm..

With the Moon entering your zodiac sign, you should grasp the chance of progress and open up new possibilities in more than one sphere of your life. You need to be in the fast lane now and won't have much sympathy with those who find it difficult to keep up. Scorpio is on a roll so make sure that everyone notices.

24 FRIDAY
Moon Age Day 7   Moon Sign Scorpio

am ....

pm..

Whatever your personal ambitions might be, this is the time to go for it. There is tremendous scope for relaxation today and for spending a few hours enjoying yourself. For Scorpio this might be as simple as a protracted stay in a comfortable hammock or it could be climbing a mountain.

25 SATURDAY
Moon Age Day 8   Moon Sign Sagittarius

am ....

pm..

Confidence grows regarding a plan that has taken up a good deal of your time already. In a social sense, your hopes tend to be fired up now. There are some interesting people about and you may find yourself making contact with someone who is going to prove especially important and fortunate in your life.

26 SUNDAY
Moon Age Day 9   Moon Sign Sagittarius

am ....

pm..

This could well be a day on which getting things done in a practical sense isn't going to be particularly easy, so you may as well relax. If you insist on starting new projects you will probably only have to begin again later so you may as well spend some time planning and try to do it somewhere really pleasant.

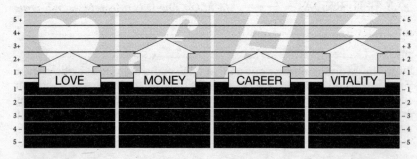

27 MONDAY
Moon Age Day 10   Moon Sign Capricorn

am ....

pm ....

People generally seem to be interested in you and are only too willing to put themselves out on your behalf. Romantic attachments should be starting to look slightly more exciting today. If you are searching for new attachments of almost any sort you could do worse than looking around at the start of this week.

28 TUESDAY
Moon Age Day 11   Moon Sign Capricorn

am ....

pm ....

You now show great determination when faced with matters that would once have held you back severely. Keep away from substances you know you have reacted against in the past and try for a healthy life. You should enjoy being on the move right now and will be starting everything as you mean to go on, particularly at work.

29 WEDNESDAY
Moon Age Day 12   Moon Sign Aquarius

am ....

pm ....

This is a day when you should think about relaxing as much as you can manage. A situation of conflict in a personal sense makes it difficult for you to stay on the easy terms with a specific individual that you might wish. Maybe you are reacting too strongly to some state of affairs that really isn't actually important?

30 THURSDAY
Moon Age Day 13   Moon Sign Aquarius

am ....

pm ....

Bringing an atmosphere of peace and harmony to your surroundings is not at all difficult right now. For the moment, diplomacy seems to be your middle name and solving disputes is your present greatest skill. Romance should figure prominently in your life around this time and your popularity is high.

31 FRIDAY
Moon Age Day 14   Moon Sign Pisces

am ....

pm ....

If you are involved in any form of education, the time is now coming to really commit yourself to it. There is much to be gained in the coming months if you concentrate on what you have taken on, and this applies whether or not education is part of the scenario. Friends might need special help.

1 SATURDAY
Moon Age Day 15   Moon Sign Pisces

am ....

pm ....

Friends could be especially demanding once again, with relatives less so. It is unlikely that you would turn down any reasonable request today, especially when the people asking are particularly well liked. You will need to keep yourself busy, if only because so much is expected of you by others.

2 SUNDAY
Moon Age Day 16   Moon Sign Pisces

am ....

pm ....

On the romantic front, you might find overtures coming in that will both surprise and delight you at some stage later on. News and information that comes in today is well worth your attention. There are potential gains on the way but you could miss them if you don't keep your eyes and ears open.

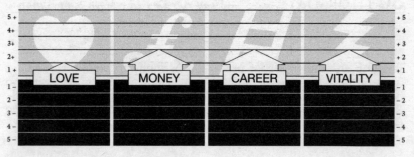

September 2012

YOUR MONTH AT A GLANCE

⊕ = Opportunities are around   ⊖ = Be on the defensive   ● = Life is pretty ordinary

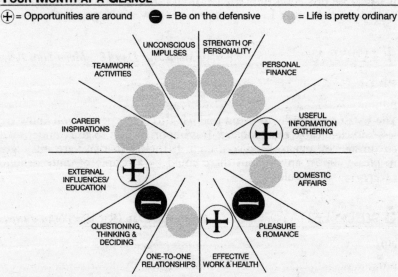

- UNCONSCIOUS IMPULSES
- STRENGTH OF PERSONALITY
- TEAMWORK ACTIVITIES
- PERSONAL FINANCE
- CAREER INSPIRATIONS
- USEFUL INFORMATION GATHERING
- EXTERNAL INFLUENCES/ EDUCATION
- DOMESTIC AFFAIRS
- QUESTIONING, THINKING & DECIDING
- PLEASURE & ROMANCE
- ONE-TO-ONE RELATIONSHIPS
- EFFECTIVE WORK & HEALTH

SEPTEMBER HIGHS AND LOWS

Here I show you how the rhythms of the Moon will affect you this month. Like the tide, your energies and abilities will rise and fall with its pattern. When it is above the centre line, go for it, when it is below, you should be resting.

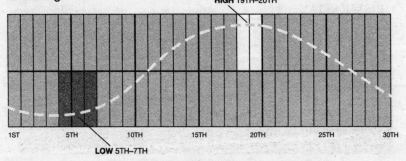

HIGH 19TH–20TH

1ST   5TH   10TH   15TH   20TH   25TH   30TH

LOW 5TH–7TH

MONDAY
Moon Age Day 17   Moon Sign Aries

am ....

pm ....

Although you are willing to offer timely advice to anyone in your immediate vicinity, you could find that at least some of your opinions are neither looked for nor welcome. Remain patient. Your capacity for personal success is on the increase, even if this doesn't necessarily show very much right now. In the main you are now working for later on.

4 TUESDAY
Moon Age Day 18   Moon Sign Aries

am ....

pm ....

You won't take kindly to being told what to do by people you know are less knowledgeable than you are. It is important not to react under such circumstances, but to keep your cool. It is clear that you are still eager to please almost anyone but there could be a couple of quite definite exceptions to the rule.

5 WEDNESDAY
Moon Age Day 19   Moon Sign Taurus

am ....

pm ....

Planetary trends suggest you will probably feel the need to withdraw from the world a little today and tomorrow. This is nothing extraordinary and it is to be expected when the Moon is in your opposite sign of Taurus. Spending time with those you love the most might seem to be the most comfortable pastime for you right now.

6 THURSDAY
Moon Age Day 20   Moon Sign Taurus

am ....

pm ....

There are limitations around at the moment and you don't have very much choice but to accept that they exist. The lunar low certainly won't get you down too much this time around because you have a strong supporting influence too. Avoid trying to prove your capabilities to others today as you may fail.

7 FRIDAY
Moon Age Day 21   Moon Sign Taurus

am ....

pm..

Although you can't necessarily make the professional progress you are seeking, you can get what you want from most situations that involve family, friends or people you have recently met. You have considerable charm and you can exercise it on the most important people in your life over the next few days.

8 SATURDAY
Moon Age Day 22   Moon Sign Gemini

am ....

pm..

If you want to get your own slice of good fortune, you need to put yourself in the way of it. This means keeping an eye on what is happening around you and taking decisive action when you see an opportunity. Luck is with you if you act quickly. Routines are not for you today or tomorrow.

9 SUNDAY
Moon Age Day 23   Moon Sign Gemini

am ....

pm..

Things should be looking good. Socially and romantically, you should find plenty of fortunate opportunities. Romance figures prominently in your thinking over the next few days but the freedom-loving tendencies are still quite evident. What you might need most of all is a change of scene and the chance to leave routine far behind.

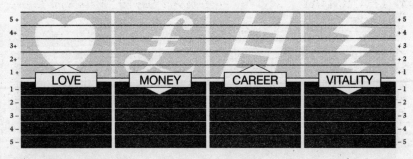

10 MONDAY
Moon Age Day 24   Moon Sign Cancer

am ....

pm..

Listen to casual acquaintances – they have plenty to say to you around now, some of which is very interesting. You definitely have the desire to spread your wings and although this might not be possible during a normal working day, there does not appear to be anything to prevent you planning ahead.

11 TUESDAY
Moon Age Day 25   Moon Sign Cancer

am ....

pm..

You may be coming to the end of a specific phase in your planning and that means deciding which direction to take next. It is very important to check and double-check all facts and figures that have a bearing on the practical side of your life today so don't take anything for granted.

12 WEDNESDAY
Moon Age Day 26   Moon Sign Cancer

am ....

pm..

Whether or not you surprise them, the most important factor is that you can steal a march on some of your competitors. Now is the time to show what you are made of. It's almost certain that others, and your colleagues especially, won't expect you to be quite as assertive today as you can sometimes be.

13 THURSDAY
Moon Age Day 27   Moon Sign Leo

am ....

pm..

There is just a possibility that you will be viewing some matters in a slightly less than sensible way today. This is particularly likely to be the case when it comes to practical considerations that also have an emotional content. Maybe it would be good to seek out the advice of an impartial observer?

14 FRIDAY

Moon Age Day 28   Moon Sign Leo

am ....

pm...

Although your commitment to hard work might not be what it usually is, you do know very well how to have a good time, something that a few of your friends might have forgotten for now. Social and romantic issues could have some extra sparkle today and there isn't much doubt that you are at your best when in company.

15 SATURDAY

Moon Age Day 29   Moon Sign Virgo

am ....

pm...

It might seem as though very few people are offering the sort of emotional or personal support you need this weekend but the fact is that you are probably looking in the wrong direction. You need to organise yourself today and to focus on issues you see as being particularly important for the future.

16 SUNDAY

Moon Age Day 0   Moon Sign Virgo

am ....

pm...

Someone you don't see very often could be coming along to take a more important position in your life. There might be a tendency to overlook minor, although vital, details at present. You need to be fully in charge of your own thought processes and only rely on advice up to a certain point.

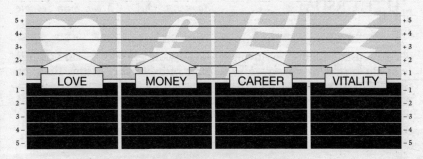

17 MONDAY
Moon Age Day 1   Moon Sign Libra

am..

pm..

Those who were once simply casual acquaintances now stand a chance of becoming good friends. The level of your optimism increases and a host of planetary alterations begin to make themselves known. Mercury, now in a strong position for you, can bring a definite interest in education and a desire to better yourself in some way.

18 TUESDAY
Moon Age Day 2   Moon Sign Libra

am..

pm..

Your warm smile, apparent optimism and great determination might be all you need to get through some adverse situations and to win out handsomely. Even when you feel you are up against it, you need to push forward and to let everyone know just how much you are enjoying life. Also, do what you can to support a friend.

19 WEDNESDAY
Moon Age Day 3   Moon Sign Scorpio

am..

pm..

Be prepared to stick your neck out in situations where you know your attitude is sensible and your desires modest. Few people will deny you what you ask for. The lunar high should help you significantly and offers a greater degree of confidence, which comes along at just the right time to pursue new successes.

20 THURSDAY
Moon Age Day 4   Moon Sign Scorpio

am..

pm..

It might be worth taking on some new responsibility at this time, or else making yourself available to help out a friend. Whatever you do at present, you should really show your style. Look out for a day or two of high vitality when you can get a great deal done in a very short space of time.

21 FRIDAY
Moon Age Day 5   Moon Sign Sagittarius

am ....

pm..

All things considered, this would be an extremely good day for mixing business with pleasure. Not everyone wants to be in your company, though those who don't are likely to be naturally miserable and would only depress you. This is a period during which you can afford to concentrate on those whose company you enjoy.

22 SATURDAY
Moon Age Day 6   Moon Sign Sagittarius

am ....

pm..

Don't worry if you find you are out of your depth on some occasions because help is at hand. It might seem easier to take shortcuts today but in the end that would only cause you more problems. By far the best way forward is to do fewer jobs but to do them to the very best of your ability.

23 SUNDAY
Moon Age Day 7   Moon Sign Capricorn

am ....

pm..

There are some less than thrilling influences around in terms of your love life. The fact is that you are not making quite the impression you might have wished and as a result you could become disappointed. The planetary influences causing this are short term in nature, so hang in there and be patient.

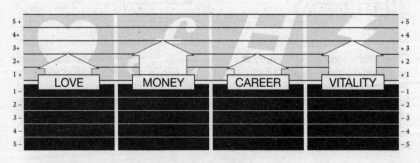

24 MONDAY
Moon Age Day 8   Moon Sign Capricorn

am ....

pm ....

Your curiosity should be in gear as you go through today on the lookout for people who can open your mind to a world of new possibilities. Start to formulate some interesting plans for the remainder of the week. The time should feel right for exploring fresh fields and pastures new.

25 TUESDAY
Moon Age Day 9   Moon Sign Aquarius

am ....

pm ....

You should have the confidence to act, especially in matters of the heart. The kindest side of your nature is uppermost and you should be willing to put yourself out considerably for others. This should enhance your popularity and mean that everyone will want you around. For the next few days, your primary concern is likely to be freedom of choice.

26 WEDNESDAY
Moon Age Day 10   Moon Sign Aquarius

am ....

pm ....

Opt for a change in domestic routines if you can today and show strong support for family members. Scorpio is much in demand at present and that means you could be spreading yourself rather too thinly. Don't try to be all things to all people because it won't work. When you are being yourself, those around you find you excellent company.

27 THURSDAY
Moon Age Day 11   Moon Sign Aquarius

am ....

pm ....

It shouldn't be hard to find the right words to tell someone how much you think about them. The reaction you get in return is likely to be far beyond your expectations and brightens this part of the week no end. Social matters work out well but it is in the area of your love life that the real gains can be made.

28 FRIDAY
Moon Age Day 12   Moon Sign Pisces

am ....

pm...

Not everyone has your best interests at heart so use your intuition to decide who to trust. Relatives and even friends might be only too willing to lend a timely hand or give advice if you ask, but in the end you have to decide things for yourself and that's something that comes easily today.

29 SATURDAY
Moon Age Day 13   Moon Sign Pisces

am...

pm...

Keep life light and easy and you won't feel in any way restricted. The fact is that quite a few issues will look very different even by tomorrow. Some sense of urgency exists regarding emotional matters, though you will be best advised not to get into deep discussions for the next day or two.

30 SUNDAY
Moon Age Day 14   Moon Sign Aries

am ....

pm...

A great day to be active and enterprising from the moment you get out of bed. Dealing with routine tasks is less of a problem than might have been the case yesterday. Social inclinations are strong. You should aim to get on with a number of different jobs at the same time while you can.

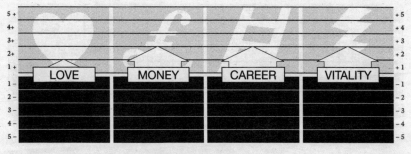

♏

October

2012

YOUR MONTH AT A GLANCE

⊕ = Opportunities are around   ⊖ = Be on the defensive   ⬤ = Life is pretty ordinary

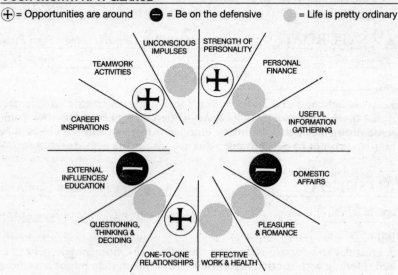

UNCONSCIOUS IMPULSES

STRENGTH OF PERSONALITY

TEAMWORK ACTIVITIES

PERSONAL FINANCE

CAREER INSPIRATIONS

USEFUL INFORMATION GATHERING

EXTERNAL INFLUENCES/ EDUCATION

DOMESTIC AFFAIRS

QUESTIONING, THINKING & DECIDING

PLEASURE & ROMANCE

ONE-TO-ONE RELATIONSHIPS

EFFECTIVE WORK & HEALTH

OCTOBER HIGHS AND LOWS

Here I show you how the rhythms of the Moon will affect you this month. Like the tide, your energies and abilities will rise and fall with its pattern. When it is above the centre line, go for it, when it is below, you should be resting.

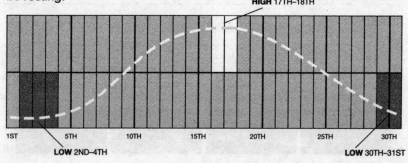

HIGH 17TH–18TH

1ST   5TH   10TH   15TH   20TH   25TH   30TH

LOW 2ND–4TH

LOW 30TH–31ST

1 MONDAY
Moon Age Day 15   Moon Sign Aries

am..

pm..

Although you can sometimes be slightly shy in settings with which you are not familiar, this won't be the case at the moment. Put yourself in good company for the start of this week. With newer and better invitations leading you down paths you didn't expect, you will need to be on the ball today.

2 TUESDAY
Moon Age Day 16   Moon Sign Taurus

am..

pm..

It looks as though Scorpio is in a slightly disagreeable frame of mind today and if you are not careful, you could get on the wrong side of someone whose friendship you would be better to cultivate. It's fair enough that you don't want to allow yourself to be walked on but there are limits which you should not ignore.

3 WEDNESDAY
Moon Age Day 17   Moon Sign Taurus

am..

pm..

Take life how it comes and don't try to change things too much. Mentally write the word 'relax' on the inside of your mind and look at it as much as you can today. It won't be very long before you can once again push for the things you really want in life but for the moment you must be patient.

4 THURSDAY
Moon Age Day 18   Moon Sign Taurus

am..

pm..

You won't feel in the least comfortable when you are forced down paths that are not of your own choosing. Give and take in romantic attachments is another key to success at present, so be willing to look at an alternative point of view when necessary. Looking for greater freedom is what makes you happiest today.

5 FRIDAY
Moon Age Day 19   Moon Sign Gemini

am ....

pm...

Success at work comes quite naturally for you now and you are able to prove your worth in a number of new ways. It's certain you are being watched, both in a professional sense and socially. People respect your point of view now and are more inclined to show it than you may have found of late.

6 SATURDAY
Moon Age Day 20   Moon Sign Gemini

am ....

pm...

Although this isn't the most rewarding time for relationships, you are likely to be attracted to some fairly unusual types, probably because you are in a slightly rebellious frame of mind. Contacts with others in social situations could prove to be either distracting or annoying, depending on who they are.

7 SUNDAY
Moon Age Day 21   Moon Sign Cancer

am ....

pm...

It is the presence of those around you that makes for such a happy time, or at least that's the way it seems to you. In reality, you are doing more than your share. Your work can be very rewarding today and this applies every bit as much to Scorpios who are in full-time education or even voluntary pursuits.

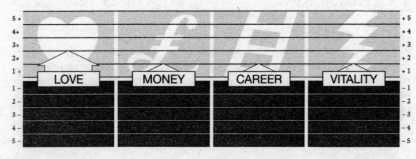

8 MONDAY
Moon Age Day 22 Moon Sign Cancer

am ....

pm..

Don't hold back today – when you have an idea, speak out. Although prevailing trends make this slightly difficult until tomorrow, necessity demands your involvement. You need to assert yourself in a creative way if you are going to get the attention of people who really matter around this time.

9 TUESDAY
Moon Age Day 23 Moon Sign Cancer

am ....

pm..

There are potential gains coming from a number of different directions, some of which might prove rather surprising. Relatives can be quite demanding. You need to support your actions with sensible attitudes at the moment, even if some other people don't fully understand the way your mind is working.

10 WEDNESDAY
Moon Age Day 24 Moon Sign Leo

am ....

pm..

Because your domestic life has rarely been better than it is likely to be right now, you may experience a conflict of interest as to what you should do. On the one hand your friends are demanding your presence and attention, whilst at home situations look warm and inviting. You will have to split your time somehow.

11 THURSDAY
Moon Age Day 25 Moon Sign Leo

am ....

pm..

Avoid getting involved in pointless disputes with people who don't really figure in your life at all. There is little time for pointless details today. The general situation at work should be improving for most Scorpios and you should be well able to let others know exactly how you feel about anything.

12 FRIDAY

Moon Age Day 26   Moon Sign Virgo

am ....

pm..

Little worries regarding family members probably turn out to be nothing of any real importance, so avoid them if you can. You are certainly in a good position to make things happen now and should be willing to lend your assistance to those you see as being somehow less well off than you are.

13 SATURDAY

Moon Age Day 27   Moon Sign Virgo

am ....

pm..

The emphasis ought to be on your creative abilities, particularly with things around the house. Making yourself feel more comfortable with your surroundings is important. You may also discover that you are basically more restless than you might have expected to be at this time.

14 SUNDAY

Moon Age Day 28   Moon Sign Libra

am ....

pm..

Communication issues seem to go quite well and you shouldn't be in the mood to be a shrinking violet at this stage of the month. You could easily be in the mood for shopping and will have a good nose for a bargain. Scorpio can sometimes be quite quiet but today you can haggle with the best of them.

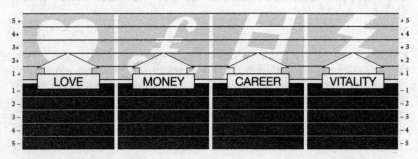

15 MONDAY
Moon Age Day 0   Moon Sign Libra

am...

pm...

Friends are especially supportive and are likely to be singing your praises, but you shouldn't find it difficult to live up to their expectations. It would be a good time to address family dealings or negotiations, and if there is something particular you want to ask for, you should chance your arm at this time.

16 TUESDAY
Moon Age Day 1   Moon Sign Libra

am...

pm...

You seem to be most interested in personal freedom and should try to avoid being fettered in any way. This is a trend that extends well into the week and the fact that you won't necessarily follow a party line is going to surprise others. It is important to explain yourself around now.

17 WEDNESDAY
Moon Age Day 2   Moon Sign Scorpio

am...

pm...

If you cultivate the right attitude, you could achieve many of the objectives you have set yourself more quickly than you expected. That doesn't mean you should rush your fences because a little care and attention is still necessary. What you should register today is how much luck is obviously on your side.

18 THURSDAY
Moon Age Day 3   Moon Sign Scorpio

am...

pm...

Although you might not consider yourself lucky with money as a rule, this could be the exception. In terms of relationships, romance is never far from the surface for some days to come. Material issues are mostly inclined to work out well for you so financial decisions can be made now with confidence.

19 FRIDAY
Moon Age Day 4   Moon Sign Sagittarius

am...

pm...

Financial gains are possible, even if these seem to come despite your own best efforts and not because of them. Keep in touch with colleagues who can be of specific practical use to you. There could be good news coming in from far and wide, some of which you should find either exciting or at least joyful.

20 SATURDAY
Moon Age Day 5   Moon Sign Sagittarius

am...

pm...

You should be able to find plenty of entertaining diversions coming from friends, many of whom definitely have your best interests at heart. Professionally speaking, you may decide that you cannot afford to miss out on anything today so keep your eyes open for opportunities.

21 SUNDAY
Moon Age Day 6   Moon Sign Capricorn

am...

pm...

Scorpio may be slightly reticent to say no at present but there are occasions when it is necessary, so you can't avoid it. At home you should feel fairly comfortable with necessary alterations. Don't make promises you can't keep. It would be better to be honest from the start, rather than having to apologise later.

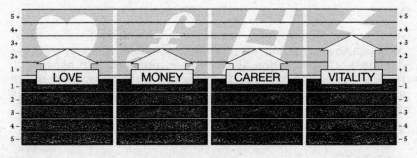

22 MONDAY
Moon Age Day 7   Moon Sign Capricorn

am ....

pm ....

Some of your victories will be hard won but the fact that you get there in the end is what counts. You have good persuasive powers today and shouldn't give in simply because someone seems to be saying no at first. This is the time when it helps to put in that extra bit of effort that can make all the difference.

23 TUESDAY
Moon Age Day 8   Moon Sign Aquarius

am ....

pm ....

Don't be too modest today and when you are asked for your opinion, do your best to act as though you have the right to offer it. You should put yourself in situations where you can be noticed because there are plenty of people watching you, some of whom are deeply attracted to that magnetic Scorpio nature.

24 WEDNESDAY
Moon Age Day 9   Moon Sign Aquarius

am ....

pm ....

As far as the intellectual stakes are concerned, you are now on top form. It is highly unlikely that anyone would be able to pull the wool over your eyes and it is clear that you know what you want from life. Friends should be instrumental in helping you achieve a particularly longed-for objective.

25 THURSDAY
Moon Age Day 10   Moon Sign Pisces

am ....

pm ....

There are some gains to be made now, not least in terms of the way you are looking at romantic matters. Don't get sucked into the complicated schemes of someone you already know is a control-freak. Seek change and variety for its own sake today and don't allow yourself to be held to one spot or one way of thinking.

26 FRIDAY

Moon Age Day 11   Moon Sign Pisces

am ....

pm ....

You have a real talent for communication and this fact is showing stronger than ever at the moment. Someone you haven't seen for a while is likely to pay a return visit to your life and could be bringing some surprises. Getting to grips with a job you don't like will be quite tedious but still necessary.

27 SATURDAY

Moon Age Day 12   Moon Sign Aries

am ....

pm ....

Superiors and those higher up the professional tree might have annoyed you during the last few days and this could play on your mind. However, if you have the weekend to yourself, put such matters to one side and concentrate on having a good time. There is any number of people around who will help you do so.

28 SUNDAY

Moon Age Day 13   Moon Sign Aries

am ....

pm ....

Optimism remains in plentiful supply for the majority of Scorpio subjects. You can be the life and soul of any party and should also be arranging some yourself. Comfort and security come as a definite second for now because what really matters is simply getting out there and finding excitement.

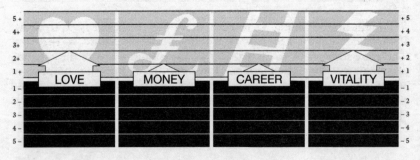

29 MONDAY

Moon Age Day 14   Moon Sign Aries

am ....

pm..

Consideration and concern are now your middle names. This is particularly the case with family members, but friends will also be on the receiving end of your concern. This would be a good time to put your sympathy into action to help out those around you.

30 TUESDAY

Moon Age Day 15   Moon Sign Taurus

am ....

pm..

This is not really a good time to compete. You are not in a very go-getting frame of mind and you would also feel sorry for your adversary, which would take the edge off your potential success. Settle for a happy time personally and maybe do a little travelling if you can today.

31 WEDNESDAY

Moon Age Day 16   Moon Sign Taurus

am ....

pm..

Take a back seat from the main action and let others deal with the decisions. You can accept that this is a time for taking a step back and for planning or you can pointlessly chase your tail. Fighting against the lunar low is like trying to push water up a hill. It isn't worth the effort.

1 THURSDAY

Moon Age Day 17   Moon Sign Gemini

am ....

pm..

You might not be feeling particularly brave but you don't need to show that to others – keep it to yourself and people will be convinced that you are the bee's knees. Don't be too quick to step aside in favour of someone else. Current trends leave you with new directions to travel, either in a real or a figurative sense.

2 FRIDAY
Moon Age Day 18   Moon Sign Gemini

am ....

pm...

Not everyone displays the same sense of humour that you do but that doesn't matter because you will make them laugh in one way or another. Look after your cash in the afternoon and evening. You should find yourself on the right side of some interesting situations today, even if you have to dream them up for yourself.

3 SATURDAY
Moon Age Day 19   Moon Sign Gemini

am ....

pm...

Good conversation is something you really enjoy this weekend and you can also have a stronger influence on the actions of your partner or family members than you might have been expecting. There are possible new rewards around most corners. A significant mental boost makes itself felt around this time.

4 SUNDAY
Moon Age Day 20   Moon Sign Cancer

am ....

pm...

It might feel as though not everyone believes in you but the people who matter the most will, and that fact is enough to see you through one or two potentially sticky moments. You will be attending to a number of different jobs today but with application, it is possible to keep all the balls in the air at the same time.

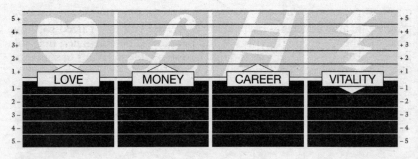

November

2012

YOUR MONTH AT A GLANCE

⊕ = Opportunities are around   ⊖ = Be on the defensive   ● = Life is pretty ordinary

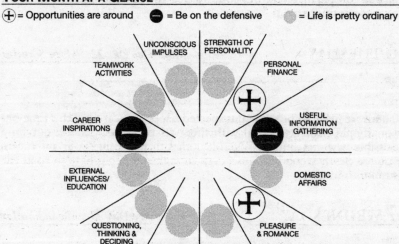

- UNCONSCIOUS IMPULSES
- STRENGTH OF PERSONALITY
- TEAMWORK ACTIVITIES
- PERSONAL FINANCE
- CAREER INSPIRATIONS
- USEFUL INFORMATION GATHERING
- EXTERNAL INFLUENCES/ EDUCATION
- DOMESTIC AFFAIRS
- QUESTIONING, THINKING & DECIDING
- PLEASURE & ROMANCE
- ONE-TO-ONE RELATIONSHIPS
- EFFECTIVE WORK & HEALTH

NOVEMBER HIGHS AND LOWS

Here I show you how the rhythms of the Moon will affect you this month. Like the tide, your energies and abilities will rise and fall with its pattern. When it is above the centre line, go for it, when it is below, you should be resting.

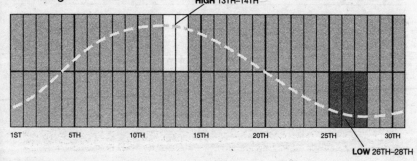

HIGH 13TH–14TH

1ST   5TH   10TH   15TH   20TH   25TH   30TH

LOW 26TH–28TH

5 MONDAY
Moon Age Day 21   Moon Sign Cancer

am ....

pm...

You are getting on well with just about everyone, even if there are one or two awkward types around. Creative potential is especially good and some of you may be thinking about redecorating. A boost to teamwork and all co-operative ventures comes along and you should make the most of these positive trends.

6 TUESDAY
Moon Age Day 22   Moon Sign Leo

am ....

pm...

There are likely to be some unexpected happenings around this time but you should manage to deal with them relatively easily. Look out for a possible new attachment. When it comes to furthering your ambitions, you are clearly second to none, even though you might have to enlist the support of others.

7 WEDNESDAY ☿
Moon Age Day 23   Moon Sign Leo

am ....

pm...

In social and family situations, you are clearly putting everyone ahead of yourself, which isn't unusual for Scorpio. Self-confidence in professional matters is definitely the way forward and you won't get anywhere if you fail to show those around you that you know what you are talking about.

8 THURSDAY ☿
Moon Age Day 24   Moon Sign Leo

am ....

pm...

It may be a good time to spend some of your social hours with people you don't see very often. It would also be a good day for sending letters or making a long-distance phone call. Close companions may now cause you to think quite deeply about the importance you have recently placed upon relationships.

9 FRIDAY ☿ *Moon Age Day 25   Moon Sign Virgo*

am...

pm...

If someone talks to you in private, you should respect their confidences. Friends are likely to be particularly demanding of your time and that won't leave quite as many hours as you might have wished for practical matters. New life can be breathed into situations you thought were over and done with.

10 SATURDAY ☿ *Moon Age Day 26   Moon Sign Virgo*

am...

pm...

Although you might not feel you have the confidence of family members, they are likely to back you when it really counts. Don't get involved in pointless rows. You might prove to be far too impetuous regarding the decisions you are making today and do need to think carefully about most matters.

11 SUNDAY ☿ *Moon Age Day 27   Moon Sign Libra*

am...

pm...

You actively want to show how capable you are and could even display a fairly intrepid quality. This is not evident all the time, so enjoy the moment. Avoid letting others get hold of the wrong end of the stick as far as your opinions are concerned. It's important to keep your eyes open for new and renewed professional opportunities.

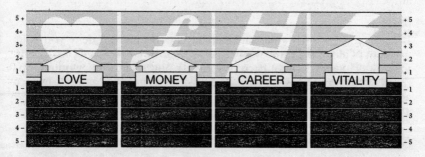

12 MONDAY ☿ *Moon Age Day 28   Moon Sign Libra*

am..

pm..

All things considered, your professional life should be on the up around now. It might be both necessary and prudent to take instructions from people who clearly know what they are talking about. The problem is that their odd behaviour might somehow reflect on you in the eyes of others.

13 TUESDAY ☿ *Moon Age Day 0   Moon Sign Scorpio*

am..

pm..

This is definitely the time to let your light shine. There are gains to be made in just about all the areas of your life and a cheerful attitude on your part that gets you into the good books of people who really count. Personality-wise you are willing to throw caution to the wind, which makes you even more attractive.

14 WEDNESDAY ☿ *Moon Age Day 1   Moon Sign Scorpio*

am..

pm..

What a great time this is to get new plans out in the open and working for you. Friends and relatives alike should be only too willing to lend a hand, the more so because your personality is so bubbly at present. Getting on with just about anyone is as easy as pie.

15 THURSDAY ☿ *Moon Age Day 2   Moon Sign Sagittarius*

am..

pm..

Because you are such a pleasant person, few people will deny you your moment of glory and those who prove awkward are not worth considering for now. Things you have been waiting for now seem to be working out the way you would wish. You have shown both patience and persistence and this shows.

16 FRIDAY
☿ *Moon Age Day 3   Moon Sign Sagittarius*

am ....

pm...

The end of a working week may also bring you to a specific decision that has been pending for ages. Friends should prove helpful now. Long-term ambitions and major aims are likely to be within easier reach at this stage. Your future is now more definitely in your own hands than seems to have been the case for a while.

17 SATURDAY
☿ *Moon Age Day 4   Moon Sign Capricorn*

am ....

pm...

Ordinary, casual encounters with friends and associates should improve significantly as the day progresses. When it comes to personal encounters, you might not have all it takes to make the best of impressions today. If, for example, you were thinking of popping the question, you should avoid doing so until at least tomorrow.

18 SUNDAY
☿ *Moon Age Day 5   Moon Sign Capricorn*

am ....

pm...

You won't find it easy to conform to expectations but you are so good to know that people won't care. On the contrary, it is your unorthodox way of doing things at present that appeals the most. Your day can be filled with promise, plus a good deal of excitement, if you are in the market for it.

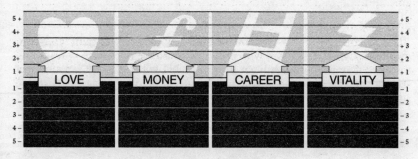

19 MONDAY ☿ *Moon Age Day 6   Moon Sign Aquarius*

am ....

pm ....

Do your very best today to be positive and to display that strong level of confidence that has been impressing others so much. However, a certain amount of caution is indicated, particularly when it comes to close personal encounters. This could be because the strong desire to get ahead is forcing you to do things you might otherwise shy away from.

20 TUESDAY ☿ *Moon Age Day 7   Moon Sign Aquarius*

am ....

pm ....

Scorpians who are self employed might prove to be the luckiest of all under present circumstances. It's a time for fast thinking and for instant action. If you are quick off the mark you can make progress in a number of different directions and might gain quite a reputation on the way.

21 WEDNESDAY ☿ *Moon Age Day 8   Moon Sign Pisces*

am ....

pm ....

Most people will gladly follow your lead now, even though it is obvious to you that you are making up your mind as you go along. The sheer magnetism of your personality is on display, and you can use that to your advantage. Your persuasive powers are strong and if there is something you particularly want to do, now is the time to get cracking.

22 THURSDAY ☿ *Moon Age Day 9   Moon Sign Pisces*

am ....

pm ....

Telling others the way you feel should be quite easy, not least because you are in a very truthful frame of mind. People you probably haven't seen for ages return to your life quite soon. You could make this a particularly good day when it comes to career matters as well as affairs of the heart.

23 FRIDAY ☿ *Moon Age Day 10   Moon Sign Pisces*

am ....

pm ....

Personal relationships take up some of your time later in the day and might promote one or two genuine surprises. It is important to mix your natural sense of personal space with an ability to get on well in group situations. This is a juggling act that you won't find too difficult to address right now.

24 SATURDAY ☿ *Moon Age Day 11   Moon Sign Aries*

am ....

pm ....

If you believe that someone is trying to dupe you, or a person you care about, the chances are that you will insist on having your say. Just make sure you have your facts right before you begin to shoot from the hip because you are unlikely to be too interested in diplomatic niceties.

25 SUNDAY ☿ *Moon Age Day 12   Moon Sign Aries*

am ....

pm ....

Once again you are showing that you won't stand any nonsense and you certainly won't take much persuading to get involved in a family row. This can be quite an explosive interlude in terms of some relationships, though generally speaking not those that are closest to your heart.

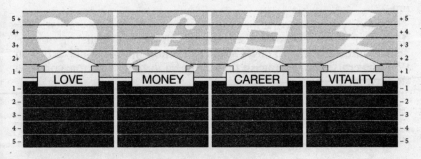

26 MONDAY ☿ *Moon Age Day 13 · Moon Sign Taurus*

am ....

pm..

Put a brake on ambitions. For the next two days the lunar low is going to slow you down in any case and there is really no point in fighting against the odds. Instead, do what you can to enjoy yourself and be ready to act in three or four days time, when the situation improves.

27 TUESDAY ☿ *Moon Age Day 14 Moon Sign Taurus*

am ....

pm..

Without too much justification, you could be feeling anxious about matters that are beyond your control but you shouldn't worry about things if you can't do anything to change circumstances. Let events unfold and everything will turn out fine.

28 WEDNESDAY *Moon Age Day 15 Moon Sign Taurus*

am ....

pm..

There are occasions when it is just as good to stand and watch life as it is to take part and this might be just such a time. Finances should strengthen a little. You might feel there is something missing about today, maybe because you never quite get into gear, especially in a practical sense.

29 THURSDAY *Moon Age Day 16 Moon Sign Gemini*

am ....

pm..

The more you talk to people today, the less likely you are to bottle things up. Younger family members may prove especially supportive. This could be a day of highly charged emotions for some Scorpios. What sets this off probably isn't remotely important – it's how you react that matters.

30 FRIDAY
Moon Age Day 17   Moon Sign Gemini

am...

pm...

You will be anxious to spread your wings and to vary your lifestyle significantly. New and interesting ways of contacting the world at large occur to you at any time around now. Routines could seem somewhat tedious and you are better off searching for the new and glitzy.

1 SATURDAY
Moon Age Day 18   Moon Sign Cancer

am...

pm...

You can appear to be very confident, even on those occasions when nothing could be further from the truth. Scorpio shows a distinct fascination for anything unusual around this time. Potential benefits come from travel, change, alternative interests and simply fascinating the people you mix with.

2 SUNDAY
Moon Age Day 19   Moon Sign Cancer

am...

pm...

You may feel considerable concern for the underdog and will continue to do so for some days. Romance can play a part in your day, especially if you are in the market for a new attachment. Be as sensitive as you can to the moods of others and make the effort to show just how caring you can be if you put your mind to it.

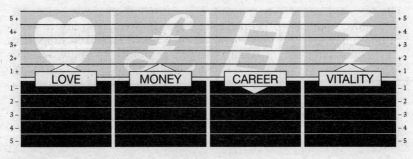

December

2012

YOUR MONTH AT A GLANCE

⊕ = Opportunities are around   ⊖ = Be on the defensive   ⬤ = Life is pretty ordinary

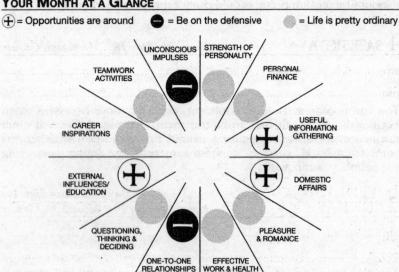

UNCONSCIOUS IMPULSES

STRENGTH OF PERSONALITY

TEAMWORK ACTIVITIES

PERSONAL FINANCE

CAREER INSPIRATIONS

USEFUL INFORMATION GATHERING

EXTERNAL INFLUENCES/ EDUCATION

DOMESTIC AFFAIRS

QUESTIONING, THINKING & DECIDING

PLEASURE & ROMANCE

ONE-TO-ONE RELATIONSHIPS

EFFECTIVE WORK & HEALTH

DECEMBER HIGHS AND LOWS

Here I show you how the rhythms of the Moon will affect you this month. Like the tide, your energies and abilities will rise and fall with its pattern. When it is above the centre line, go for it, when it is below, you should be resting.

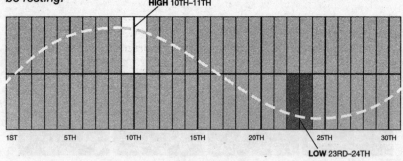

HIGH 10TH–11TH

1ST   5TH   10TH   15TH   20TH   25TH   30TH

LOW 23RD–24TH

150

3 MONDAY *Moon Age Day 20   Moon Sign Cancer*

am ....

pm ....

Try not to be pushed into anything now because in the end you need to choose for yourself. There is probably more time than you think and plenty of chance to check a few details with people who are in the know. Pressure to get things done could be evident, particularly at work.

4 TUESDAY *Moon Age Day 21   Moon Sign Leo*

am ....

pm ....

You could find that a good way to spend today would be by looking below the surface of what is going on and proving how perceptive you can be by getting to the heart of a matter. The events unfolding around you could bring a little more excitement but also a puzzle or two.

5 WEDNESDAY *Moon Age Day 22   Moon Sign Leo*

am ....

pm ....

People who don't figure in your life very often are now likely to put in an appearance and there are gains coming along if you pursue a generally progressive and go-ahead attitude. On a professional level this would be a good time to arrive at agreements and compromises.

6 THURSDAY *Moon Age Day 23   Moon Sign Virgo*

am ....

pm ....

Creative potential is especially good and allows you to also make changes at home. Some last-minute but important information could lead to a change of plan. Fortunately, you are one of the most adaptable signs of the zodiac so altering things isn't difficult and doesn't create too many stresses.

7 FRIDAY

Moon Age Day 24   Moon Sign Virgo

am ....

pm..

There are gains to be made from helping family members, even if these are really only in terms of your self-esteem. Although material rewards are few today, personal happiness should be strong. Use a little cheek and take the chance that is offered to ask for what you want and make sure you retain command of situations.

8 SATURDAY

Moon Age Day 25   Moon Sign Libra

am ....

pm..

If you show a generous spirit today, no matter what you are doing, this will increase your popularity and cement your friendships. There is nothing new about your behaviour at present. Probably the only difference is that others are now paying more attention than usual.

9 SUNDAY

Moon Age Day 26   Moon Sign Libra

am ....

pm..

There could be a few niggling doubts around but don't allow these to get in your way. Avoid getting involved in a complicated home-based situation. Social relationships should prove to be very exciting and your efforts to make the best possible impression should be worthwhile.

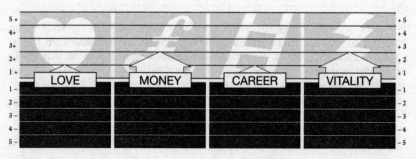

10 MONDAY   *Moon Age Day 27   Moon Sign Scorpio*

am ....

pm ....

Now you are really in gear and your lunar-high focus is almost certainly going to be on Christmas. There are many practical things to be done and even if you have been very organised you will find more. Dashing about from pillar to post is definitely no problem as far as you are concerned.

11 TUESDAY   *Moon Age Day 28   Moon Sign Scorpio*

am ....

pm ....

It is better to be on the move this week and to travel as much as you can. You are clearly curious about the world right now and keen to see as much of it as possible. If there are any restrictions placed on you at the moment, these probably exist more in your head than in reality.

12 WEDNESDAY   *Moon Age Day 0   Moon Sign Sagittarius*

am ....

pm ....

New initiatives are on the cards, so you might want to make changes around your home to improve your long-term comfort. This should make for an interesting period that could be more eventful than you expect. This is a good time for get-togethers, particularly with people you don't see all that often.

13 THURSDAY   *Moon Age Day 1   Moon Sign Sagittarius*

am ....

pm ....

Patience is a virtue that you have in cartloads today so make sure this is your greatest ally. Work developments should favour you at this time, with extra responsibility probably bringing greater rewards. If these don't arrive right now, you can expect them over the medium and longer term.

14 FRIDAY
Moon Age Day 2   Moon Sign Capricorn

am ....

pm ....

This is a very special time of year as far as you are concerned and you like to have everything as organised and comfortable as possible. In terms of relationships you ought to be feeling very secure at present, which is a definite advantage with Christmas only just around the corner.

15 SATURDAY
Moon Age Day 3   Moon Sign Capricorn

am ....

pm ....

People are well disposed towards you so hone in on that and you can make a very good impression, even on strangers. There are financial gains to be made, so look out for a special bargain. Display an optimisitic face and you should find that personal ambitions and hopes turn out pretty much as you would expect.

16 SUNDAY
Moon Age Day 4   Moon Sign Aquarius

am ....

pm ....

Not everyone is quite so willing to see your point of view today, which is why you have to show the high degree of diplomacy of which your zodiac sign is so capable. In personal relationships, aim for the sort of mutual understanding that you know will make this part of December less of a hassle.

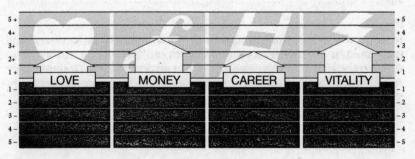

17 MONDAY
Moon Age Day 5   Moon Sign Aquarius

am ....

pm ....

With Christmas only a week or so away there is likely to be something you are not happy about. Pitch in and change circumstances for the best chance of overall contentment. If you feel a certain restlessness, just wait for it to pass – it is not unusual or significant.

18 TUESDAY
Moon Age Day 6   Moon Sign Aquarius

am ....

pm ....

Don't leave travel plans to chance but make sure that all details are sorted well in advance. This might be a journey you intend to take today or perhaps even as late as Christmas itself. The quickening pace around you in everyday life now shows at every turn and you will barely have time to breathe right now.

19 WEDNESDAY
Moon Age Day 7   Moon Sign Pisces

am ....

pm ....

You are likely to be much more involved with money than might normally be the case, even if the necessities of the holiday season may get in your way. Today is a period of smiles. Property and financial interests are now very well highlighted and will continue to be so for the rest of the month.

20 THURSDAY
Moon Age Day 8   Moon Sign Pisces

am ....

pm ....

It seems that others find you extremely entertaining to have around and they could be making you feel like a celebrity at the moment. Confidences come in thick and fast, some of them from directions you certainly would not have expected. Mental inspiration can come your way via travel and social discussions.

21 FRIDAY

Moon Age Day 9   Moon Sign Aries

am...

pm...

Avoid getting into pointless discussions about things that don't matter. Some people might describe you as being too assertive but if they do it's probably only because they are used to getting their own way. All that is happening is that you know what you want from life and are more than willing to say so.

22 SATURDAY

Moon Age Day 10   Moon Sign Aries

am...

pm...

Although you might not have too much professional influence on a Saturday, there are ideas coming into your mind at the moment that you will act on after the holidays. You can capitalise on new opportunities and won't be stuck when it comes to expressing your opinions, no matter who is on the receiving end.

23 SUNDAY

Moon Age Day 11   Moon Sign Taurus

am...

pm...

There are possible delays around at the moment and little you can do about the situation. Although you are doing everything you can to get ahead, the world seems determined to throw obstacles in your path. All you have to do is to relax for today and wait for better trends to arrive after the lunar low.

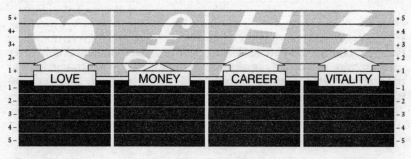

24 MONDAY   *Moon Age Day 12   Moon Sign Taurus*

am ....

pm ....

There need to be moments during the day in which you can simply stand and look, both at your handiwork and at the world at large. This is particularly true if you have small children whose attitude to Christmas you can share. Dashing about all the time is no way to fully enjoy what Christmas Eve has to offer you.

25 TUESDAY   *Moon Age Day 13   Moon Sign Gemini*

am ....

pm ....

This is not a Christmas Day during which to force anything. You get on best today if you go with the flow, though only up to a point. If people are really behaving in an outrageous manner, you are likely to tell them. You won't gain any enemies this way because practically everyone wants to listen to what you have to say.

26 WEDNESDAY   *Moon Age Day 14   Moon Sign Gemini*

am ....

pm ....

You show a very definite urge to impress people and you may also desire travel at some stage today. There is a degree of restlessness that has to be addressed in one way or another. Current influences keep you involved socially and make sure this is not simply a family-motivated Boxing Day.

27 THURSDAY   *Moon Age Day 15   Moon Sign Gemini*

am ....

pm ....

Finances could begin to look stronger than you imagined. Mentally speaking you remain fairly restless and will need to ring the changes if you are not to become frustrated. You could join forces with those around you who are feeling equally dynamic in order to make the best possible impression that you can.

28 FRIDAY
Moon Age Day 16   Moon Sign Cancer

am ....

pm ....

Don't get too tied up with details today because it is clearly the overall picture that is important at present. A job you have been involved with for quite some time could be nearly over.

29 SATURDAY
Moon Age Day 17   Moon Sign Cancer

am ....

pm ....

Some Scorpio patience is called for today. You feel like working hard to get what you want from life, but not everyone is in the same frame of mind as you are.

30 SUNDAY
Moon Age Day 18   Moon Sign Cancer

am ....

pm ....

All is happiness around you and if you have been a little restricted by the negative attitude of friends or family members, this sort of situation is now likely to be disappearing.

31 MONDAY
Moon Age Day 19   Moon Sign Leo

am ....

pm ....

With a recognition of the needs of those around you, it is possible to have everything fully on course for a splendid evening that everyone can enjoy. All the same, at the very end of the year, your love life might prove to be slightly problematic.

	LOVE	MONEY	CAREER	VITALITY
5 +				+5
4 +				+4
3 +				+3
2 +				+2
1 +				+1
1 -				-1
2 -				-2
3 -				-3
4 -				-4
5 -				-5

RISING SIGNS FOR SCORPIO

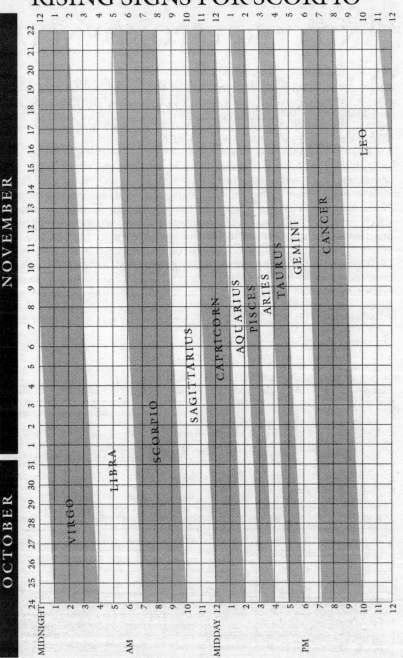

THE ZODIAC, PLANETS AND CORRESPONDENCES

The Earth revolves around the Sun once every calendar year, so when viewed from Earth the Sun appears in a different part of the sky as the year progresses. In astrology, these parts of the sky are divided into the signs of the zodiac and this means that the signs are organised in a circle. The circle begins with Aries and ends with Pisces.

Taking the zodiac sign as a starting point, astrologers then work with all the positions of planets, stars and many other factors to calculate horoscopes and birth charts and tell us what the stars have in store for us.

The table below shows the planets and Elements for each of the signs of the zodiac. Each sign belongs to one of the four Elements: Fire, Air, Earth or Water. Fire signs are creative and enthusiastic; Air signs are mentally active and thoughtful; Earth signs are constructive and practical; Water signs are emotional and have strong feelings.

It also shows the metals and gemstones associated with, or corresponding with, each sign. The correspondence is made when a metal or stone possesses properties that are held in common with a particular sign of the zodiac.

Finally, the table shows the opposite of each star sign – this is the opposite sign in the astrological circle.

Placed	Sign	Symbol	Element	Planet	Metal	Stone	Opposite
1	Aries	Ram	Fire	Mars	Iron	Bloodstone	Libra
2	Taurus	Bull	Earth	Venus	Copper	Sapphire	Scorpio
3	Gemini	Twins	Air	Mercury	Mercury	Tiger's Eye	Sagittarius
4	Cancer	Crab	Water	Moon	Silver	Pearl	Capricorn
5	Leo	Lion	Fire	Sun	Gold	Ruby	Aquarius
6	Virgo	Maiden	Earth	Mercury	Mercury	Sardonyx	Pisces
7	Libra	Scales	Air	Venus	Copper	Sapphire	Aries
8	Scorpio	Scorpion	Water	Pluto	Plutonium	Jasper	Taurus
9	Sagittarius	Archer	Fire	Jupiter	Tin	Topaz	Gemini
10	Capricorn	Goat	Earth	Saturn	Lead	Black Onyx	Cancer
11	Aquarius	Waterbearer	Air	Uranus	Uranium	Amethyst	Leo
12	Pisces	Fishes	Water	Neptune	Tin	Moonstone	Virgo